Music Business Marketing

James Bruce

Published by James Bruce, 2024.

While every precaution has been taken in the preparation of this book, the publisher assumes no responsibility for errors or omissions, or for damages resulting from the use of the information contained herein.

MUSIC BUSINESS MARKETING

First edition. March 4, 2024.

Copyright © 2024 James Bruce.

ISBN: 979-8224544103

Written by James Bruce.

Table of Contents

Chapter 1...1

Chapter 2...6

Chapter 3.. 12

Chapter 4.. 16

Chapter 5.. 21

Chapter 6.. 26

Chapter 7.. 31

Chapter 8.. 35

Chapter 9.. 44

Chapter 10 47

Chapter 11 50

Chapter 12 52

Chapter 13 58

Chapter 14 65

Chapter 15 69

Chapter 16 75

Chapter 17 86

Chapter 18 91

Chapter 19 95

Chapter 20 100

Chapter 21 110

Chapter 22 119

Chapter 23 122

Chapter 24 126

Chapter 25 135

Chapter 26 148

Chapter 27 155

Chapter 28 173

Chapter 29 178

Chapter 30 186

Chapter 31 194

Chapter 32 203
Chapter 33 211
Chapter 35 223
Chapter 36 231
Chapter 37 238
Chapter 38 246
Chapter 39 253
Chapter 40 261
Chapter 41 268
Chapter 43 280
Chapter 44 288
Chapter 45 293

Chapter 1

How to Create a Successful YouTube Channel for Music Sales

1. Setting up your YouTube Channel

To create a successful YouTube channel for music sales, there are a few essential steps you need to follow. First, choose a catchy channel name that reflects your music brand and appeals to your target audience. Next, create an appealing channel banner that visually represents your music style and captures viewers' attention. Optimize your channel description with relevant keywords to improve search results and attract more visitors. Selecting an eye-catching profile picture is also crucial for branding and recognition. Once your channel is set up, focus on creating engaging content that resonates with your audience and encourages them to stay connected. Promote your channel and music sales through various platforms to expand your reach and attract more potential buyers. Finally, regularly analyze and improve your channel's performance by tracking metrics and adjusting your strategies accordingly.

1.1 Choosing a catchy channel name Choosing a catchy channel name is crucial for the success of your YouTube channel. A catchy name will grab the attention of potential viewers and make your channel memorable. When choosing a channel name, consider your target audience and the genre of music you will be promoting. It should reflect your style and be unique. Research to ensure that the name you choose is not already in use by another channel. Aim for a name that is easy to pronounce and spell, as this will make it easier for viewers to find you.

1.2 Creating an appealing channel banner Creating an appealing channel banner is an essential step in setting up your YouTube channel for music sales. Your channel banner is the first thing viewers will see when they visit your channel, so it should be eye-catching and visually appealing. It is important to choose high-quality images and graphics that reflect the style and genre of your music. Consider including your logo or artist name, as well as any relevant images or artwork that represent your brand. Be sure to use consistent branding across your channel banner, profile picture, and thumbnails to create a cohesive and professional look. Remember, your channel banner is like a billboard for your music, so make it engage and enticing for viewers.

1.3 Optimizing your channel description for search to optimize your YouTube channel description

for search, it is essential to include relevant

keywords and phrases that relate to your music niche. This will help potential viewers discover your channel more easily. Additionally, make sure to provide a concise and compelling overview of your channel's content, highlighting the unique aspects that set it apart from others. Use clear and concise language to convey your channel's value and encourage viewers to subscribe. Lastly, consider including links to your social media profiles and websites to increase visibility and provide viewers with additional ways to connect with you.

1.4 SELECTING AN EYE-catching profile picture Selecting an eye-catching profile picture is crucial for attracting viewers to your YouTube channel. Your profile picture is the first thing that viewers see when they come across your channel, so it needs to be visually appealing and representative of your music. Choose an image that captures the essence of your brand and stands out from the competition. Consider using a high-quality and professional-looking photo or logo that is easily recognizable. Keep in mind that the profile picture will also appear as a small thumbnail, so make sure it is clear and distinct even at a smaller size. An eye-catching profile picture will help to create a positive and memorable impression, increasing the likelihood of attracting viewers and boosting your music sales.

2. Creating Engaging Content

To create engaging content for your YouTube channel, it is important to focus on quality and variety. Firstly, ensure that the audio and video production of your music videos is of high quality to capture the attention of viewers. Experiment with diverse types of content, such as tutorials, behind-the-scenes footage, or interviews, to keep your audience interested and coming back for more. Incorporating storytelling and personal anecdotes into your videos can also help to create a connection with your viewers. Additionally, encourage audience participation by asking for feedback, hosting contests, or featuring fan-submitted content. Lastly, consistency in posting the latest videos and engaging with comments and messages from your viewers will help to build a loyal community around your channel.

3. Promoting Your Channel and Music Sales Promoting Your Channel and Music Sales: To maximize your channel's visibility and drive music sales, start by leveraging social media platforms to share your content and engage with your audience. Collaborating with other popular music YouTubers can also help you reach a wider audience. Additionally, create a consistent posting schedule and use relevant keywords in your video titles and descriptions to improve search visibility. Encourage viewers to subscribe, like, and share your videos, and consider running targeted ads to reach potential fans. Lastly, analyze your channel's performance using YouTube analytics and make data-driven improvements to optimize your content strategy and increase music sales.

4. Analyzing and Improving Performance Analyzing and improving performance is a crucial aspect of running a successful YouTube channel for music sales. This section will explore various tools and strategies to track your channel's performance and identify areas for improvement. By analyzing key metrics such as views, likes, comments, and subscriber growth, you can gain valuable insights into what content resonates with your audience the most. Additionally, understanding audience demographics and behavior can help you tailor your content and promotional strategies accordingly. This section will also discuss techniques for optimizing your videos for search, utilizing analytics platforms, and implementing strategies to enhance engagement and increase music sales. By continuously analyzing and improving your channel's performance, you can maximize your reach and profitability on YouTube.

Chapter 2

Tips for YouTube Promotion

1. Creating Engaging Content

Creating engaging content on YouTube is crucial for attracting and retaining viewers. By utilizing storytelling techniques, YouTubers can captivate their audience's attention and create a connection with them. Incorporating humor and entertainment into videos can also make them more enjoyable and shareable. Another effective strategy is showcasing unique perspectives or experiences, as this can set a creator apart from their competition and make their videos more memorable. Overall, focusing on creating engaging content is the foundation for a successful YouTube promotion strategy.

1.1. Utilizing storytelling techniques Storytelling is a powerful technique that can engage and captivate your YouTube audience. By crafting narratives and incorporating compelling narratives into your videos, you can create a more personal and relatable experience for viewers. Use storytelling techniques to draw your audience in, evoke emotions, and keep them invested in your content. Develop characters, set up conflicts, and resolve them to create a compelling narrative arc. Utilizing storytelling techniques can help you establish a unique voice and differentiate yourself from other YouTube creators.

1.2. Incorporating humor and entertainment When it comes to YouTube promotion, incorporating humor and entertainment can be a meaningful change. By injecting a dose of laughter and amusement into your content, you can capture the attention of viewers and keep them engaged. Whether it is through funny skits, witty commentary, or clever editing, adding humor can make your videos more memorable and shareable. Entertainment value not only attracts a wider audience but also encourages viewers to stay on your channel and watch more of your content. So do not be afraid to embrace your comedic side and bring a smile to the faces of your viewers.

1.3. Showcasing unique perspectives or experiences When promoting your YouTube channel, it is important to showcase unique perspectives or

experiences. This helps you stand out from other creators and attract a dedicated audience. Share your personal stories, insights, or expertise in your videos to provide viewers with valuable and engaging content. By offering a fresh and unique perspective, you can captivate your audience and keep them coming back for more. Do not be afraid to experiment with different formats or approaches to make your content even more distinct. Ultimately, showcasing your unique perspectives or experiences will help you build a loyal following and increase your channel's visibility and success.

2. Optimizing Video Titles, Descriptions, and Tags Crafting attention-grabbing titles is an essential aspect of optimizing video promotion on YouTube. A captivating title can entice viewers to click on your video, increasing its visibility and potential reach. Additionally, writing comprehensive video descriptions that accurately summarize the content can improve search visibility and provide viewers with a clear understanding of what to expect. Utilizing relevant and targeted tags is another effective strategy for optimizing video promotion. By including keywords and phrases that are related to your video's content, you can increase the chances of your video appearing in relevant search results. Optimizing video titles, descriptions, and tags is crucial for enhancing the discoverability and overall success of your YouTube channel.

2.1.   Crafting   attention-grabbing   titles   Crafting attention-grabbing titles is crucial for successful YouTube promotion. A catchy and intriguing title can grab viewers' attention and entice them to click on your video. To create attention-grabbing titles, consider using strong and descriptive words that clearly convey the content of your video. Keep your titles concise and to the point, while still creating curiosity. Additionally, using numbers or asking questions in your titles can also attract viewers. Experiment with different title formats and analyze the performance of your videos to identify what type of titles resonates best with your audience.

2.2. Writing comprehensive video descriptions When writing video descriptions for YouTube, it is important to be comprehensive and provide as much information as possible. This includes including relevant keywords, a summary of the video's content, and any additional links or resources. By writing detailed video descriptions, you can improve your searchability and attract more viewers to your channel. Additionally, consider using closed captions and transcripts to increase search visibility and accessibility for a wider audience.

2.3. UTILIZING RELEVANT and targeted tags Utilizing relevant and targeted tags is a key aspect of YouTube promotion. By choosing the right tags for your videos, you can increase their visibility and reach a wider audience. When selecting tags, consider the keywords that are relevant to your content and that your target audience is likely to search for. It is important to be specific and use tags that accurately describe the topic of your video. Additionally, research popular tags in your niche and incorporate them into your videos to increase their discoverability. By utilizing relevant and targeted tags, you can improve your video's chances of being recommended to viewers and increase your overall visibility on YouTube.

3. Leveraging Social Media Platforms To maximize YouTube promotion, leveraging social media platforms is crucial. One effective strategy involves sharing videos on popular platforms like Facebook, Instagram, and Twitter to reach a wider audience. Engaging with the YouTube community through comments and collaborations also helps to build a strong following. Additionally, utilizing hashtags strategically can increase discoverability and attract more viewers to your content. However, it is important to balance self-promotion with genuine engagement and valuable contributions to the community. By leveraging social media platforms, you can significantly enhance your YouTube promotion efforts and increase the visibility of your videos.

3.1. SHARING VIDEOS on Facebook, Instagram, and Twitter

In the section "Sharing videos on Facebook, Instagram, and Twitter," you will learn strategies for promoting your YouTube videos on these popular social media platforms. By sharing your videos on Facebook, Instagram, and Twitter, you can reach a wider audience and increase your video's visibility. These platforms provide opportunities to engage with your followers, share updates about your latest videos, and leverage the power of social sharing to expand your reach. By utilizing these platforms effectively, you can attract more viewers to your YouTube channel and grow your subscriber base. Additionally, sharing your videos on social media allows you to connect with your audience on a more personal level and build a community around your content. Implementing these strategies will help you effectively promote your YouTube videos and drive more traffic to your channel.

3.2. Engaging with the YouTube community through comments and collaborations

Engaging with the YouTube community through comments and collaborations is an essential aspect of YouTube promotion. By responding to comments on your videos, you can show appreciation for your audience's feedback and foster a sense of community. This engagement can also lead to increased visibility for your videos, as active participation in the comments section can encourage viewers to share and like your content. Furthermore, collaborating with other YouTubers can help expand your reach by tapping into their existing audience. Collaborations can take the form of guest appearances on each other's channels or creating joint content. By actively engaging with the YouTube community, you can build a loyal following and increase your chances of success on the platform.

3.3. UTILIZING HASHTAGS strategically to increase discoverability

Utilizing hashtags is a keyway to increase discoverability on YouTube. By incorporating relevant and popular hashtags into your video titles, descriptions, and tags, you can make it easier for users to find your content. Researching and selecting the right hashtags that align with your video's topic and target audience is essential. Additionally, it is important to use hashtags that are trending or frequently searched for to increase your chances of being discovered. By utilizing hashtags strategically, you can expand your reach and attract more viewers to your YouTube channel.

4. Implementing Effective SEO Strategies

To implement effective SEO strategies for YouTube promotion, it is crucial to conduct keyword research to optimize your videos. By understanding what people are searching for, you can tailor your content to fit those keywords and increase your visibility in search results. Another useful tactic is to utilize closed captions and transcripts for improved search visibility, as they provide additional textual information about your video's content. These strategies will help you rank higher in search results and attract more viewers to your channel.

4.1. Conducting keyword research for video optimization
Conducting keyword research is a crucial step in optimizing videos for YouTube. By identifying popular and relevant keywords, you can increase the likelihood of your videos being discovered by your target audience. Start by brainstorming keywords and topics related to your video content, then use keyword research tools to analyze their search volume and competition. Look for keywords with high search volume and low competition to maximize your chances of ranking well in search results. Incorporate these keywords naturally in your video titles, descriptions, and tags to improve your video's visibility and attract more viewers. Additionally, consider using closed captions and transcripts to further optimize your video for search engines.

4.2. Utilizing closed captions and transcripts for improved search visibility
Closed captions and transcripts are valuable tools for improving search visibility on YouTube. By providing closed captions, you make your videos more accessible to a wider audience, including those with hearing impairments. Transcripts also give search engines more content to index and understand the context of your videos. This can lead to higher rankings in search results, making your videos more discoverable. Additionally, utilizing closed captions and transcripts can help you target specific keywords and phrases, further boosting your search visibility. By incorporating these strategies into your YouTube promotion, you can increase the reach and impact of your videos.

Chapter 3

Using social media

You can use social media for:

Personal reasons: For dating, to find friends with similar interests, to track the current "chatter" about a topic that interests you. The possibilities are limitless.

Customer Service: You can create a company account and let people know that they can send questions or concerns to this account, and you can respond via Twitter or Facebook instead of by email. You can update customers on upcoming news or events (sales, problems, news, product recalls, etc.).

Public Relations: Develop relationships with media reps, reporters, and bloggers. Media are big users of Twitter, and it is a wonderful place to connect and build relationships. Facebook is also an effective way to connect and interact (so is LinkedIn and various other industry-specific sites)

Growing your business: Drive traffic to your website, build relationships, make exclusive offers, and monitor your brand (make sure you are searching Twitter and Facebook for your name and your company name so you can be aware of what is being said about you - respond promptly and accordingly to what you find during your monitoring). You can promote events, exclusive offers, and new products, services, or tools. You can use social media to establish yourself as a credible leader in your industry.

Here are some tips that I think you will find especially useful.

Offer Quality content - This is a cornerstone of your business. It determines your credibility. If you cannot put out something of quality, you will not get far. You do not have to have every answer and cover every point in your articles, posts, and tweets. But you need to put thought, you need to organize it well, and it needs to appear professional and polished. It needs to say something or mean something, and it needs to be something that you are proud to have to speak for you publicly because that is what your content does (tweets, posts, articles etc.). Remember that every piece of content you put online via whatever vehicle is like an employee walking around talking to people and networking for you. Would you send out a guy who smells, cannot answer questions, did not brush his hair or tuck in his shirt, and is so self-absorbed he can only converse when it is centered around his needs? Nope, I sure hope you will not. So do not put out stinky content that pushes your agenda without offering something of value. Specifically, that means creating a balance of information that you put out there, you have to put out calls to action and sales messages, so balance that out with helpful tips, motivational questions (people love retweeting those), and some newsworthy tweets about your region (it helps establish your local presence and local companies are more likely to promote you if they think you are an advocate and source of information for that region)

Offer Unique Content - There is only so much that can be said about a topic BUT that does not mean that you cannot put your unique spin on it. Think about how to present it in a way that stands out to others. They may hear something twenty times and on the 21st time, they get it. So, it may not be a discovery you are reporting but you are putting your unique spin on it. Please don't misunderstand, retweeting and reposting other quality content is important too, and again it's the spirit of social media - but in addition to that you need to add your unique material to the conversation, or you just become a vehicle for other people's content, and you don't build credibility and exposure for your own.

Offer value - This one is a no-brainer, and it is where most people drop the ball. You need to offer something of value. It could be a discount, it could be info, it could be a good laugh, it could be an answer to a question, it could be advice or news. There are so many ways to offer value. One of the best ways is to ask people what they are looking for and what they need. Survey your social media followers - find out what problems they have, what questions they have, what products or services they need - and then offer it to them.

Attract- I think before you can engage someone you need to first attract them. You attract them with your personality, style, wit, images, compassion, and knowledge. To me this means you must be "skim worthy" - when someone lands on your Twitter profile or even sees one tweet or post, there must be something in it that attracts them and makes them want to spend more time. Once they spend time, they will see you offer value, they will feel engaged, and they will like or share.

Engage- We talk about engaging people because we are all inundated with messages: tweets, Facebook posts, Blog posts, RSS feeds, emails, videos, and ads. The ones that people respond to are the ones that engage them. The ones that make them feel connected and feel like it speaks to them. What I talked about above on Likes and Shares is the need to engage people to get them to do the Liking and Sharing. The best way to engage is to be conversational and not formal or corporate. Also, ask questions - even benign questions like "What is your goal for today" or something like that - it gets people interacting and you cannot underestimate the importance of getting people to engage and respond. It is great if the questions are related to your industry but generic "how are you/what are your plans" kind of things help too.

Share- We talk about sharing because the goal of social media is getting people to share our content, so it spreads and creates more exposure. So, know going in that your goal is to get a share. Ask yourself if the content you are putting out there (whether it is a 140-character tweet or a

full-on Blog post) is worthy of a share. Is it funny, witty, controversial, informative, honest, shocking? Does it solve a problem or answer a question? Does it cause people to smile, laugh, gasp, question, think? Ask yourself what your reaction would be when you read that content and be sure it evokes some kind of reaction. That is how you get a retweet. Important tip - if your tweet is too long, it is hard for people to share it (retweet it) - so be sure you leave some room for the message to be retweeted. You know they are going to put RT @yourusername before the tweet, so you need enough characters for that to fit in before the message. This means if you want a lot of RTs you are dealing with less than 140 characters.

Go Viral - Note you do not need any or all your content to go viral to find success. Granted, it is the Holy Grail of the likes/shares/retweets. Everyone wants to go "viral" and see their content spread like wildfire. The stuff that usually goes viral is strong and funny, attention-getting, controversial, shocking, etc. Focus on quality content and a variety of various kinds of content (writing, video, pics, etc.) and focus on building personality, adding value, and offering unique content and you will work your way to viral.

Chapter 4

The Publicist

What Exactly Does a Publicist Do?
A celebrity publicist acts as the intermediary between the celebrity and entities who want to contact them. One of the main job responsibilities of a celebrity publicist is to generate positive media exposure while simultaneously maintaining a positive public reputation. Furthermore, a good celebrity publicist will interact with the media and other people and entities who want to contact their clients. A publicist is usually specified to one person in the entertainment industry. And that person oversees their client's overall public image. So, anything that you read about someone or watch an interview, is orchestrated and done by the publicist. Then the publicist oversees how the world preserves a certain person.

Setting Up Interviews with A Celebrity
As any tabloid will let you know, there is certainly no shortage of crises and gossip affecting entertainment stars and celebrities. As a celebrity publicist and crisis manager, spends a lot of time helping his clients get through any periods of gossip or crisis that could negatively affect their image. You used to see a lot of covering up with scandals in general. We are now seeing that does not work...so, public relations have changed drastically because we are now realizing that being honest, being transparent is not a sad thing. And so now the new generation of publicists...we are

encouraging our clients to step into the light, be more transparent, be honest, do not hide from things.

When he is not engaged in managing the crises and scandals of his clients, the publicist also spends a fair amount of time interacting with media brands that are trying to reach out to his clients. From interviews to podcasts, the publicist receives dozens of contacts every week. So how does he determine which one is a good fit for his clients?

When we get an email from a brand that wants to partner with one of our clients, even based on how we get the information depends on whether they are a good match for our client. Really what is important are the numbers, how many people listen or read per month, things like that.

While the number of viewers or listeners that a media brand can offer is certainly important, the quality of production is also a major concern. It is also based on... the level of professionalism... If I have someone who runs a podcast. They want to interview a client and they may not have a ton of listeners, but the production value of the podcast is high caliber. You know, I am much more willing to give it a shot than... a podcast that had a ton of listeners but sounds like it has been recorded out of a can.

The Logistics of Setting Up an Interview

Just because you have a high-quality podcast or YouTube channel that generates a fair number of viewers or listeners, does not necessarily mean that you are guaranteed to get an exclusive interview with a celebrity. Timing is everything if you want to successfully engage with a publicist for a celebrity you are trying to engage. If you are targeting a specific client or a specific celebrity, you should know what is happening in that world based on what the publicist is putting out. So, if they are doing interviews, try and jump in on that. If you see that they are being quiet, still reach out to kind of gauge interest, but know that chances are that the interview's not going to happen. Along with the right timing, the format for interacting with celebrities is also an important consideration that is often overlooked. While in-person interviews are usually the best option, distance often makes that impossible and phone interviews are the next best option. Usually how that works is we do a three-way call or conference call. So, I will call my client and then I will put them on hold and then call the radio station, we will just do a three-way call. And then I usually mute my phone line and I take notes in the background.

Contacting a Celebrity Publicist

The best ways to get in touch and the format for contacting publicists through email. As much information as you can lay out in one email is great for us because then we can just take that information directly to our client. A lot of what a publicist does is they are just a gatekeeper. So, we take information, we digest it, we present it to our clients and then hopefully if our client has questions, we can then answer those. Some people prefer to pick up the phone rather than sending an email, but that may not always be the best strategy. There are reasons why publicists prefer not to answer your calls. If you call, I will not expect an answer. Email is preferable. Publicists are on the phone constantly anyway, between talking to clients and talking with journalists. I get phone fatigued easily, so for me, it is simply better to have an email that I can respond to when I can. And, especially when you are dealing with any kind of money, it is nice to have those details in an email so that you can go back and refer to them later.

What to Avoid When Contacting Celebrity Publicists Of course, there are also some rules and guidelines that all media brands and marketers should abide if they want to successfully engage with a celebrity publicist. That generic email that sends out daily is driving a celebrity publicist crazy and putting you on their blacklist. Politeness still goes a long way...I mean, it is not uncommon for me to have five hundred emails a day...so I do have to prioritize and figure out: "okay, what's pressing for what client?" Sometimes the response is not always able to happen, and I try and respond to every email and inquiry to at least say, "Hey, thanks for reaching out, but this is not going to work out right now.

While being enthusiastic, persistent, and aggressive can be an excellent quality for successful media brands and marketers, there is certainly a line that should not be crossed. By far my biggest pet peeve is demanding an interview. Interviews are not paid...and depending on the season we are in; I may not need that press for the client. So, we would just be doing it as a favor to the outlet to keep up a good relationship. So, I say my number one pet peeve is people just demanding things. The big question, of course, is how often media brands and marketers can reach out to a celebrity publicist without crossing the line of annoyance. Reach out once a week for three weeks and then let it go. Any more than that would be a nuisance and then there is a good chance that after three tries there is a reason you are not getting a response. Either it is not an enjoyable time or the outlet's not the right fit.

Some Last Words of Advice

Getting a celebrity endorsement for your media brand or product is a wonderful way to get a business to grow and expand its reach. Learning the best strategies to approach celebrities through their publicists is essential if you are going to be successful. Being direct and concise are two attributes that should guide your overall strategy. Rather than us as the publicist trying to figure out how your brand works, we appreciate (when a media brand says) "Hey, this is exactly the copy we want to see on the Instagram post." That makes our job ten times easier. If you are having trouble getting your product in front of your chosen celebrity, another strategy would be to organize an event and specifically invite that celebrity. Any public appearance, paid or not paid, is handled by the publicist. So, even if it is not like a red carpet, it is just an invitation, it is a charity event, that all goes to the publicist. Alternatively, charity events are another way to create an occasion to interact with a celebrity. When we go in and start working with a client, we

determine their charitable interests, so we know which charities a good fit is. Even for charitable activities, however, being upfront and honest about your expectations is essential. We just want to know upfront what it is you are expecting of our client, so the time commitment, if they want products, what that looks like, everything up front is just helpful for us...That way we do not waste anybody's time.

Chapter 5

Promote Your Music on Twitter

If you want to promote your music on Twitter, there is enough good data out there to

inform your social media promotion efforts and help you maximize the effectiveness of each tweet.

First, schedule your tweets at peak hours to get them in front of the most eyes. Second, you want to write tweets that encourage action (retweeting, purchasing, replying, etc.)!

Promote your music on Twitter:

1. Longer tweets get more clicks. Internet marketers like to tell you to keep things short. But a tweet is only 140 characters, so it is one of the few cases online where you benefit from using all the space you are allotted.

2. Use more verbs. Fewer nouns. We are emotionally stirred by action! So, make your tweets sing, screech, punch, and dance.

3. Tweet in the afternoon and evening. After 2 pm, Twitter traffic increases dramatically. Folks feel like they have enough work done for the day that they can afford to sneak in 5 minutes on

Twitter. So, schedule your tweets with those people in mind.

4. Tweet closer to the weekend. As the workweek draws to a close, Twitter traffic soars — with Friday being the busiest day. So, your heaviest Twitter activity should be on Thursday and Friday.

5. Ask for the retweet. A lot of times in life the simplest way to get something is to ask. The same goes for Twitter. People are far more likely to retweet your content if you ask them.

6. Spread tweets out by at least 1 hour. You want to get the most people possible to see your tweets. By spreading out your Twitter activity by at least an hour, you are increasing the likelihood of different folks seeing your activity. Plus, you are not annoying your followers by cluttering up their news feeds all at once.

7. Try putting the link towards the beginning of the tweet. Sure, 60-80% of your tweets should link to interesting content. But there's also evidence to suggest that you should place that URL towards the beginning of your tweet. In many A/B tests between similar tweets, the one with the URL up front performed better.

8. Write a longer blog or post that way you can quickly tweet about it and link back to the longer

piece. For your fans to want to read your tweets, click on your links, and retweet you, they need you to be authentic. Speak your mind (respectfully of course) and be genuine – do not just push your music onto the crowds. Engage in real conversations. If you do this, you will see a vast improvement in your retweet and click-through rates.

9. Be honest. Do not be afraid to admit you do not know the answer to a question... it just shows you are human. If you do make a mistake, admit you have made one. Your fans will appreciate you even more.

10. Reply and engage in a two-way dialogue. Do not let your fans hang dry. Get in the practice of taking a few minutes every day to reply to fans. Being active and responsive not only shows you care but also motivates your fans to participate in conversation. Also, do not just tweet at your fans. Think of it as a game of tennis – do not serve the ball and disappear. Follow conversations your original tweets initiated and participate in the dialogue. Be sure to follow others on Twitter and recognize fans who tweet about your blog posts or retweet something right – honesty is the best policy.

11. Be diverse. Do not just engage in conversation, be sure to share links to other useful content. Fans really love to see

photos, videos, etc. so be sure to share those. If you do not have a music video, share a 'behind the scenes' look, or a casual interview. Be sure to post a comment along with the video or any other link. Research has proven that including and sharing links helps to grow and retain followers.

12. Drive fans to your blog and website. Do not just use Twitter as a conversation channel; use it to drive fans to your blog and/or website for additional content. One way is to provide something of value, like a new single/soundtrack download, for free.

13. Update your profile. Do not forget to update your profile. Be sure to include a link to your website, a photo of you or your band, a short

3–4-word description of your music and even the name or two of known artists you sound

like. Include a link to your music.

14. Respond to criticism. So not all tweets will be rosy, and not all tweeters will be fans – expect some brutal honesty and criticism. The challenge is how you respond to these, and you need to respond. Remember anything you or others tweet is public and is 'tattooed' onto your account, so think before you type. Acknowledge their comments and propose to take the conversation offline if necessary. If you do it properly and respectfully you may turn your critic into your biggest fan.

15. Leverage technology out there to make things easier. There are some great FREE tools out there (such as www.ho[1]otsuite.com[2]) that can save you a lot of time and boost the quality and quantity of your posts by suggesting tweets (such as holiday posts, breaking news, links to videos, articles, etc.) and automating best practice issues such as coordination across social channels, scheduling, etc. Some tools also help you set up additional channels such as a blog, a website, or a Facebook Page. While these tools by no means replace personal posts, they do help by increasing the quantity, quality, and diversity of tweets you send out.

16. Invite your friends & put the word out. So, the easiest, most natural way to get started on Twitter is to invite your real-life friends to have real-life conversations with you on Twitter. Once you get the ball rolling with your friends' things will naturally pick up and you will start reaching out to others. Also, use your gigs to promote your Twitter username and invite your audience to post photos or comments about the show. You can even include your Twitter username on posters, flyers, emails etc.

---

1.   http://www.hootsuite.com/

2.   http://www.hootsuite.com/

Chapter 6

Places to Promote Your Website Online

Whether you've already taken your business online or still looking for a simple solution to[1] create a professional website[2], you probably already know that promoting your website is crucial to your success.

If you have no previous experience with site promotion, promoting your website is not only simple but it can also be done without even spending a penny!

Check out the links below for a list of opportunities to promote your site online for free! With the right time and effort, you can find yourself attracting a whole slew of new clients

to your great-looking site!

Search Engines

It may or may not surprise you to hear that most of the traffic from the internet is derived from search engines. With that said, search engines should be the first place that you should turn to promote your online presence. Ensure that search engines know that your site exists by submitting your link directly to them. Once that is out of the way, the best way to improve your search engine

---

1. http://www.wix.com/website/templates

2. http://www.wix.com/website/templates

presence is by taking the time to improve[3] your SEO[4].

Right now, the search engines that generate the most traffic are:

Google[5] Yahoo[6] Bing[7]

Online Directories:

The modern-day Yellow Pages, online directories are where potential clients turn to find business solutions. Adding your site to online directories is extremely important as it improves your site's SEO by linking back to your website. When submitting your site, make sure to include vital details like your location and business category so that your website will appear in sub-categories where new and potential clients can easily find you.

Yelp[8]

Google [9]Business[10] Yahoo Local[11] TripAdvisor[12] Yellow Pages[13] Super Pages[14] Angie's List[15] Manta[16]

BBB[17]

---

3.   https://www.wix.com/support/html5/search-engine-optimization/

4.   https://www.wix.com/support/html5/search-engine-optimization/

5.   http://www.google.com

6.   http://www.yahoo.com

7.   http://www.bing.com

8.   https://biz.yelp.com/

9.   https://www.google.com/
business/?utm_medium=et&utm_source=gmb&utm_campaign=us-en-et-gs-z-gmb-l-z-h%7Emy%7Credirect%7Cu&gmbsrc=us-en-et-gs-z-gmb-l-z-h%7Emy%7Credirect%7Cu&ppsrc=GMBLR

10.   https://www.google.com/
business/?utm_medium=et&utm_source=gmb&utm_campaign=us-en-et-gs-z-gmb-l-z-h%7Emy%7Credirect%7Cu&gmbsrc=us-en-et-gs-z-gmb-l-z-h%7Emy%7Credirect%7Cu&ppsrc=GMBLR

11.   https://smallbusiness.yahoo.com/local-listings?s_local=add

12.   https://www.tripadvisor.com/Owners

13.   http://adsolutions.yp.com/
advertise-with-us?utm_campaign=YPR_%28direct%29&utm_medium=YPR_%28none%2
9&utm_term=YPR_&utm_source=YPR_%28direct%29_home_main_1063

14.   http://claimlisting.superpages.com/spportal/
quickbpflow.do?tsrc=SP&campaignId=SP_header

15.   http://www.angieslist.com/

16.   https://www.manta.com/ng

17.   http://www.bbb.org/council/for-businesses/

Merchant [18]Circle[19]

Social Link Building

Social sites are where many web surfers spend most of their online time. Linking your content on popular social sites is a wonderful way to put your business in the face of your known audience, and a fantastic opportunity to gain quality backlinks by exposing your brand to broader audiences.

Facebook[20] YouTube

* More than a social network, YouTube is one of the most searched business directories in America

Google +[21] Pinterest[22] Reddit[23] LinkedIn Instagram LiveJournal TikTok

Blogging Platform / Article Submission

Blogging platforms and article submission sites are a terrific way to promote your site. All you need to do is author an original article related to your business and submit it to these sites. While it is important to keep these articles informative,

18.   https://www.merchantcircle.com/
signup?utm_medium=signup&utm_source=getstarted

19.   https://www.merchantcircle.com/
signup?utm_medium=signup&utm_source=getstarted

20.   https://www.facebook.com/pages/create/

21.   http://www.google.com/+/learnmore/

22.   http://business.pinterest.com/en

23.   http://www.reddit.com/about/

Try to keep your tone friendly. Articles that sound genuinely well-intentioned and have a less aggressive marketing tone will draw more interest to your site than self-promotion alone. Blogs and articles are also great for promoting link building for SEO benefits.

Blogger[24]

Owned by Google, Blogger is hardwired with Google's AdSense advertising program.

You can also add the Blogger Feed [25]from the Wix App Market to your website for maximum exposure.

Tumblr[26] Digg[27]

Photo Sharing

Similarly, social network sites like Pinterest photo-sharing sites allow you to display visual content that is related to your business and can be used to refer and link back to your website. Photo-sharing sites are not for photographers alone – any business can use these sites to post images of events, coworkers, news, and everything in between if it is connected to your business.

---

24.   https://www.blogger.com

25.   http://www.wix.com/app-market/blogger/overview

26.   https://www.tumblr.com/

27.   http://digg.com/

Chapter 7

Start Out Locally But

You can focus your time locally and globally. If you have a manager, he will be promoting you eventually both locally and globally.

But if you over-commit yourself locally, you under-commit yourself globally, and vice-versa if you are not careful or you do not have a plan in place.

If you are local, then you are social, doing a lot of things in person, and being a part of your community. But this means you will have less time to focus on creating things for the world. Having a manager helps with that problem.

If you are global, then you want to focus on creating things that can reach out through distribution to the entire world. But this means you will have less time to be part of your local community, but if that is ok it will help get you and your music out there.

Neither is right or wrong, but you need to be aware of the choices you are making.

For me, I have worked with artists both ways and it works if you budget yourself and your money.

Your attention should always be focused outward.

Some people feel no separation. You are treated equally, no matter where you are from or who you know. There are no outsiders. If extra-strong bonds are made, it is based on who you are now -not where you came from or where you have been. A successful artist today must feel that I believe if he wants his/her music heard throughout the world.

One will feel more natural to you. Like your tendency to be an introvert vs extrovert, or conservative vs liberal, these base worldviews will shape your preferences for being local-focused or global-focused.

Building a local fanbase.

To build a local fanbase, local musical artists must perform regularly at local venues. By consistently showcasing their talent and connecting with the community, artists can gain exposure and attract potential fans. Additionally, collaborating with other local artists can also help expand their reach by tapping into the existing fanbases of their peers. Another effective strategy is utilizing social media platforms to interact with fans, share updates and preview contemporary music. By consistently engaging with their audience online, artists can create a loyal fanbase and generate buzz around their music.

Expanding beyond the local scene.

Expanding reach beyond the local scene is essential for local musical artists to gain wider recognition and success. One effective strategy is to release music on streaming platforms. By making their music available on popular platforms such as Spotify, Apple Music, and Amazon Music, artists can reach a global audience and increase their chances of getting discovered. Another way to expand reach is by engaging with online communities. Participating in music forums, social media groups, and online fan communities allows artists to connect with potential fans and industry professionals. Seeking opportunities for radio airplay is also crucial. Submitting music to local and online radio stations increases exposure and raises the chances of getting played on the air. Finally, booking regional tours is an excellent way to expand reach and gain new fans outside the local scene. Playing gigs in nearby cities or venues helps artists build a following in different areas and exposes their music to diverse audiences.

Building an online presence

Building a strong online presence is crucial for local musical artists to achieve success in today's digital age. By creating a professional website, regularly updating social media profiles, sharing engaging content, and interacting with fans, artists can establish their online presence and attract a wider audience. Utilizing these online platforms allows artists to showcase their music, connect with fans, and promote upcoming shows and releases. With the increasing popularity of streaming platforms and social media, it is essential for artists to prioritize their online presence to reach and engage with their target audience effectively.

The Music Industry

Building connections within the music industry is essential for local musical artists to achieve success. By connecting with industry professionals, artists can gain valuable insights and opportunities that can propel their careers forward. There are several ways to seek industry connections and opportunities. These include attending music conferences and networking events, submitting music to blogs and online publications, collaborating with established artists or producers, and pitching songs to music supervisors for film/TV placement. By actively engaging in these activities, local artists can increase their visibility, expand their network, and increase their chances of success in the industry.

Chapter 8

The Newspeople

Here are a few things to be concerned about when presenting your news to newspeople.

• Professionally written communications: Journalists love proficient writing, and even though this can be inherently subjective, it is something upon which a good PR campaign is founded. When communicating on subjects about which you are passionate (and if you're not basing a PR campaign on your passion in business, then you're already starting in the wrong place), your words should have rhythm, timber and pitch like symphonic music. It is not just about your message; it is about communicating it eloquently and with style. Journalists will respect that element of it, even if your message does not resonate with them.

• Tie in the News: The fact that you are launching a new product line or service is not important news to a journalist just because it is news to you. Now, if your product or service could be viewed as a solution for a problem that's getting play in the news cycle - for instance, a health problem, diet issues, credit or financial problems - then you could pitch yourself as an expert on the topic with tips on how to combat it. If you can tie your company or offering into the news cycle, you will always move to the front of the line.

• **Follow Up, But Not Too Much:** After you send a journalist a story, they appreciate a little follow up, because many of them are not exactly slaves to their incoming emails. They appreciate it even more if your follow up is respectful of their time. The temptation may be to call regularly to see if they are interested in what you sent them, but rather, keep your communications focused and concise without calling too often. Even if they turn down your current pitch, they will be more likely to pay attention to future communications from you.

• **Give Them News:** A lot of companies use every excuse to send out a press release, because they think it will keep them on the press radar. However, the press is far more interested in quality of news than quantity. Be choosy when communicating with them and only send items that would be of interest to their readers. If you respect the journalist's job description - which is to report the news - the journalist will sense that. The real pros are familiar with the dance. They know you are promoting something commercial when you reach out to them, but if you help serve their readers' need for useful and timely information that is helpful to them, the reporter will not mind so much. It is the classic trade-off that makes the media work.

• **Be Gracious When They Turn You Down:** Just getting a journalist to read your release or your pitch does not mean they will say yes and do the story. If they are not interested it could be for a variety of reasons. It might be because of a busy news cycle, or simply because they have just run a similar piece, or it could be that they just do not see the news value in your pitch. No matter what, the key to motivating them to read your NEXT release is to be gracious when they turn you down. Even if reporters are a little snippy with you, take the high road and simply respond politely and graciously, thanking them for the time they gave you. Remember, they are on deadline and are dealing with daily pressures to deliver the news. Moreover, their job is the only one in which their mistakes are printed and circulated to tens of thousands, with their names at the top for all to see. If they are a little short with you, do not take it personally. If you maintain a professional, polite demeanor with them, they will be more likely to keep reading your pitches and releases, and they will be more motivated to work with you when you send them something that IS interesting to them.

The Press Release

A press release is a document outlining some sort of news, put forth by you, intended to share that news with the media and the public.

As you proof-read your press release, you check to make sure all the essential elements are there: attention-grabbing headline, well-articulated news angles, dateline written in AP style, tightly written introductory paragraph that includes all five "W's," a quote from a company executive, company boilerplate paragraph, contact information for media seeking more information. Now, here are five elements to take your press release beyond basic and help it stand out from the crowd and resonate with your targeted media. All these elements offer additional context and make it easier to tell and understand the story.

1. Third-party quotes - everyone expects to read a quote from someone in the company who is spinning the news in a positive light. But another quote, from a third-party, can make your news stand out in two ways: readers are interested in who is being quoted and in what they are saying. The quote can come from a celebrity, customer, analyst, or someone whose opinion is respected in your business industry. If it is a customer or partner endorsing you or the product, their quote can explain the unique reason they like you or, better yet, quantify the success they have had with your help. If you are using the additional quote to name-drop, be sure to give the "celebrity" something to say- when they endorse you or your news, explain what their connection or involvement is. Similarly, respected professionals in the industry can give weight to your story by offering a quote that explains what you bring to the industry that others do not.

2. Links to social media - make your text-only document come alive with hyperlinks to more content or ways to share and manage your story. As a first step, make sure there are appropriate hyperlinks within your news announcement, then offer standard "side" links so readers can easily share your news, e.g., a universal share icon to Tweet or Email the news to friends, a "Digg this" link, etc. Take it a step further by linking to a del.icio.us page with more hyperlinks and notes to relevant content sources, providing context and ongoing updates. Include a link to your online newsroom or blog so readers can view comments, participate in discussions on the topic see other relevant links, and offer RSS and email options to your blog.

3. Connection to an event - if the news is being unveiled at a tradeshow, mention the booth where you will be exhibiting so people can find you and pay a visit. If the news coincides with a tour or photo op, mention that and invite the media to attend to get more mileage out of it. Giving your news additional hooks, such as in-person, local touchpoints, makes it tougher to resist and easier for media to determine which beast or writer is most interested in your news.

4. Artwork or downloadable extras - wherever appropriate, be sure to include links to podcasts, videos, photos, screen shots, graphs, surveys, PowerPoint presentations, white papers, or online polls.

5. Spin - I know, I know...we call these news releases and regularly advise PR writers to eliminate hype and

hyperbole. But, done the right way, adding "spin" or context can help sell your story to the media. In this case, think like an editor. Why would a writer be interested in your news? If it is not immediately obvious, you may need to broaden your story's appeal by explaining how it impacts consumers, industry, the local region, etc.

And if you want results

More key components you need to have in place if you want to get results with your press release marketing.

1. Commitment to long-term distribution - In the past, I have talked about the magic bullet theory of public relations. This theory says that all you need to get the attention of journalists is one press release. Of course, that is a load of BS. Just one press release will rarely get the job done. Many journalists do not trust companies they do not know much about, so you must work on building familiarity with them. That is where long-term distribution can help. By sending out press releases regularly, you earn name recognition and increase your chances of getting coverage.

2. Knowledge of the journalists you are targeting - Too many companies take the scattershot approach to distributing their press releases. They send it out to every journalist they can find contact info for, regardless of whether that reporter is a good fit for the story. Before you send out your press release, you need to have a list of reporters who cover your industry. Those are the

ones you should be targeting. Do not waste your time on irrelevant pitches.

3. An actual plan - Don't make up your plan as you go along. Playing things by ear will get you nowhere fast. You need to produce a sound PR strategy that includes goals, plans for reaching the goals, and standards for measuring your results. Every press release you write should be designed to help you get closer to reaching your goals.

4. Knack for finding newsworthy angles - One of the most common complaints I hear is "Our company doesn't have any news to write about!" Always, this is wrong. There is always a story, you just must know where to find it.

5. Strong headlines that suck readers in - The headline of your press release usually makes or breaks the deal. A weak headline will land your press release in the trash, but a strong one could catch the eye of a busy reporter.

6. No distribution on free websites - First off, free press release distribution is not free. Finding the right directories and uploading your press release on each of them takes several hours. I am from the "time is money" school of thought, so I hardly consider this a free form of press release distribution. What is worse is these sites just do not work. Your press release will not get sent to reporters; instead, it just sits on a low-ranking directory with thousands of other press releases.

7. Follow-up skills - Reporters are a busy bunch. So, even if your press release is genuinely great, they may wind up looking at it and forgetting about it. That is why you need to know how to follow up. This helps you remind the reporter about your story, establishing rapport and keeping your company on the reporter's mind.

Chapter 9

Meet and Greet

R ule 1
Purchasing a meet and greet does not include admittance into the show.

A meet and greet is an event where fans can meet their favorite artists or bands in person. These events usually take place before or after concerts and require an additional ticket purchase or a VIP package. Meet and greets allow fans to connect with their idols on a personal level, ask questions, and express their admiration. They offer a chance to meet the artist, take photos, obtain autographs, and enhance the overall concert experience. Some meet and greets may also include early entry into the venue, a soundcheck experience, tour merchandise, and a chance to chat briefly with the artist. If you are planning to attend a meet and greet, it is important to research the artist and their music beforehand, bring a camera or autograph book, be respectful, and enjoy the moment.

How to request a meet and greet.

• 1. Go to the Artists website to purchase a meet and greet ticket or contact the venue, agent or the representative that is offering the meet and greet event.

• 2. Make sure you verify the date and time of the concert and location you will be attending.

• 3. Pay for the meeting and greet, making sure the site is secure.

• * Note your Special Needs or Requests. These include you requiring special assistance such as a wheelchair.

• You will pick up your special meet and greet at the show or as instructed by the representative. Meet and greets usually take place before the show or at such time as requested by the artist.

• 4. Be sure to pick up your pass at least 1 hour before the meet and greet or whatever time is suggested.

• FOR QUESTIONS OR SUPPORT please contact the artist or their representative.

• rules and regulations

RULES AND GUIDELINES

1) THIS DOES NOT INCLUDE ADMITTANCE INTO THE SHOW. YOU MUST PURCHASE YOUR TICKET. Each person is responsible for purchasing their admittance to the concert. You must have tickets to the show to go to the meet & greet. Meet & Greet passes do not give the member any special privileges towards parking, additional merchandise, etc.

2) A meet & greet pass is for one person. You cannot bring guests through the meet & greet line. If you would

like a friend/parent/spouse to attend the meet & greet with you, he or she will have to have purchase their own pass.

3) Certain shows (private engagements, fairs, festivals, casinos) may not allow Meet & Greet opportunities.

4) All sales are final. If you are unable to attend the meet and greet or do not make it on time, no refunds will be given. All meet and greets take place one hour prior to the show.

5) You must bring a picture I.D. with you to gain access

Chapter 10

Do and Do Nots

Do Nots

Tell them what to do.

Show up late.

The artist refuses to turn down the volume.

Fight with any patron.

Sign and return the contract.

Get drunk.

Demand too much

Send bad photos.

Send outdated or bad information.

Being phony

Send website with broken links.

Being unprepared to do business.

Miss or cancel a gig.

Badmouth anybody.

Bad first impression

Doing things that are embarrassing.

TheDos

Theoppositesofthedonotsplus:

Returnallphonecalls.

Cater to the audience.

Concern yourself with the venue making money.

Theartistthathelpswithmarketingandpublicity

Be helpful.
Be happy and have fun.
Have a positive attitude.
Look impressive.

HaveagreatEPK.

Create a press release.

Volunteerforacharity

Recognize and show appreciation.

Be well rehearsed.

Offer merchandise.

Well-choreographed.

Meet and greet.

Play the songs people want to hear.

Keep everybody in sound.

Say thank you.

Share you and your talent.

Answerfanmail

Learnthenameofyourbestfans.

Post photos of your fans

Putonagreatshow.

Seek reviews.

Try writing songs.

Joinapopularcause(notpoliticalorreligious)

Chapter 11

Music Business

NO MATTER WHAT YOU build, a framework will provide support and give it shape. In a business, the framework represents the strategies and resources you must promote and grow your business. This is no different with the music business.

If you want more than struggling musician status, then a framework will let you achieve impressive results; so that you can develop a fan base and achieve your individual music career goals.

Creating a framework for your music business plan will provide clarity and direction with which to achieve your goals. Putting this together is like a jigsaw puzzle, the framework is like the corners and edge pieces that you connect to get started.

To establish the framework, you need the following things:

An operations plan - This covers the management and development of music gigs, recordings of your work, distribution of your music and the other revenue generating areas you might pursue.

A marketing plan - This is how you will

promote your work. It might include PR distribution, flyer and poster distribution and online activities like social networking, podcasting, and video promotion.

A management plan - this is crucial to your framework, and it involves putting together a team to manage your music business well.

A finance plan - without a finance plan you will have trouble getting the other elements to hold in place. Make the effort to understand at least the basics of this side of things and you will do much better for having made the effort.

Chapter 12

Goals

• It is a new year, and a clear slate is in front of all of us. I see a marked difference between artists who set finite goals and those who do not.

Is this the year I want to make a difference in my musical career? Think of goal setting as if you were in a foreign place - You would not get where you expect to go without a clear set of directions. Goal setting is like drawing a map for yourself.

This article is designed to assist you in creating a personal roadmap for achieving what you would like with your musical career this year, whether you consider music your hobby or you are making a living out of it full-time.

Many studies have proven that the long-term perspective is the most accurate single predictor of upward social and economic mobility in America. And it has been proven that people who have goals written down are much more likely to **achieve** them.

Write Down Your Focus Areas

Here is a list of some areas you may want to focus on.

B randing Marketing Newsletter Website
Social Networking Publicity
Booking Merchandise Money
Film and TV Placements Expanding Your Fan Base Team
Time Management Writing & Recording Your Equipment
Personal Health

Write Your Goals Down

- Write each goal as if it is already happening

- Give dates by when you want to achieve each one

- Your goals should involve you and only you (they cannot be contingent on someone else)

- Make them so they are realistically achievable

- Start with small goals so I can get them checked off the list and get in momentum fast!

Look At Goals Everyday

Start With an Easy Goal and Complete It

One of the main reasons people do not end up achieving their goals / keeping their new year's resolutions is they set themselves up for failure by choosing goals that take a lot of discipline and time to achieve. There is nothing wrong with having big goals however, here is what I recommend overcoming this issue...

Choose a simple goal and achieve it within the next two weeks. This will start your momentum and get you feeling like you are in full forward motion.

Think of a small, achievable goal that only takes four to five hours to complete.

Choose something like:

o Organize cluttered studio. o Clean off desk.

o Delete unwanted files from computer. o Recycle last year's unwanted papers. o Write one new song.

Next, set a date when you will get it done by and go for it.

Now that you have achieved a goal within the first two weeks of the new year, the rest of your goal setting will seem a lot easier to accomplish, and you will be able to get things off your plate.

Make Lists to Stay on Track

• Make daily lists of what you need to do to get your goals met – the night before! Do the hardest thing first in the morning - do not procrastinate.

• Do something every day that moves you towards the goals

• Delegate the little activities that waste your valuable time to other people (you would be amazed what you could do with 4 hours it takes to clean your house).

• Do not overload yourself – studies show that six tasks are the maximum you can achieve in one day!

Get Help

Build a TEAM to help you!! Get an intern or two – log on to http://www.entertainmentcareers.net and post as an employer seeking interns – you will be amazed at how many bright young people would like to get their feet wet in the business.

If you are not comfortable with the idea of an intern, then ask a friend or a family member to help you. Schedule just 2 hours a week with that person to attack the goals and get them in motion.

Structure Time to Achieve Goals

They will not happen unless you have time to make sure they do!

Remember You Can Change the Goals as You Go

Goals should be looked at as beacons and guiding points for you to keep yourself on track along your journey. I would not recommend changing them every week, but the music industry is changing so rapidly it is hard to know what goals are reachable in this landscape. So, if the course of the year your goals change its OK to cross one off or modify as you go.

Write Down 5 Successes Each Day

I am inviting you to write down five little victories a day for this entire year. Once you start getting into this habit, you are training yourself to put the focus on the positive and get your brain to stop being so critical.

MY FINAL PIECE OF ADVICE IS – GO EASY ON YOU!

This is a process intended to take an entire year and you will have your days where you may get frustrated, and you will start to beat yourself up (sound familiar?)

Self-criticism will interfere directly with achieving your goals and dreams. So, the next time you are making yourself wrong, take a step back and instead acknowledge the good, and celebrate your achievements.

Another thing that will stop you is not taking time for YOU so schedule time to reflect and take it all in. That is a walk in the woods, which is cooking yourself a decadent meal, or it is spending time with people you love and turning down your power for a few days without the pressure of a holiday or an event....

Chapter 13

Email Marketing Best Practices

Targeted email marketing is an extremely effective way to reach your customers and drive sales. According to a recent report [1] by consulting firm McKinsey, email marketing is nearly 40 times more effective for acquiring customers than Twitter and Facebook combined.

But it is an art. You need to make sure that what you are sending is relevant and engaging (and that you do not seem intrusive). Square's Customer Engagement tool [2] gives you a solid leg up here. Because it automatically creates lists of your loyal, casual, and lapsed customers, you can make sure you are always targeting the people who will be most interested in what you are sending. One group may be more appropriate for an event invitation, for example, while another may be better suited to receive a huge sale announcement.

But beyond effective targeting, there are several email marketing dos and don'ts you should familiarize yourself with — especially if you are just dipping your toes in. Here are our top tips:

---

1. http://www.mckinsey.com/insights/marketing_sales/

    why_marketers_should_keep_sending_you_emails

2.   https://squareup.com/customer-engagement

Do not flood people's inboxes.

Think of all the emails you get in your account — and how quickly it adds up. You want to show your customers' inboxes the same respect you expect other businesses to show yours. But what is the right cadence? Not more than once a week (even if that can be a lot). A general rule of thumb is to only send an email when the content is truly engaging and worth the read. The second you send an email that is sort of "meh" for customers, you will get a slew of unsubscribes.

Avoid the spam filter.

Click Here for a Prize! WIN A FREE CRUISE! These are the types of subject lines that are likely to get caught in spam filters. So before beginning your email marketing efforts, it's a good idea to familiarize yourself with the FTC's spam laws[3]. Beyond the law, some common spam triggers include all-caps subject lines, a low text-to-image ratio, or exposing HTML in the body of the email.

Send actionable content.

With each email you send, think about the action you want your customers to take when they open it. Is it to shop for a sale? RSVP to an event? Include one actionable link (this is commonly referred to as the call to action or CTA) as the

---

3.   https://www.ftc.gov/tips-advice/business-center/guidance/can-spam-act-compliance-guide-business

centerpiece of your email. Some examples include "Shop the sale," or "RSVP here."

Timing is key.

The day of the week and the time of day you send your email can have a significant impact on these numbers, so it is worth pouring over your data to spot trends. But if you are sending your first marketing email, common sense will get you most of the way there. Think about when you are most likely to open and read your email. Typically, most people go through email in the morning, around 7 to 9 a.m. (heed the time zone). Weekdays are also better — specifically Tuesday, Wednesday, or Thursday. But there is usually also an open-rate spike on Sunday evenings when people are chilling out on the couch with their phones (Square's email templates are optimized for mobile). Make sure you time your email, so it will get noticed.

Say something enticing.

Subject lines are crucial. They are often the reason why someone opens your email or deletes it. This topic is an expansive one (we will get into it more in a later post), but your subject line should entice people to open the email to learn more. This can be accomplished in several creative ways, but simple, direct, and actionable is the way to go.

Email marketing wrongs!

Not using the signup form

This is one of the most common mistakes we see. If you do not use a signup form on your website, blog, and social channels, you are missing one of the most valuable and efficient ways to grow your list of contacts.

Not sending a welcome email: After you have your email sign-up form ready and ready to go, make sure your next step is to set up and send an automated welcome email. It should be triggered to send each time someone signs up for your list. An effective and engaging welcome email does just what it says: welcoming and thanking your new subscriber or customer. If done correctly, a welcome email can keep a recent sign-up coming back for more.

Your subject line is a snooze: Did you know the average person receives about 121 business emails a day? And that number is expected to increase. That does not even include the number of personal emails people receive. You get the picture. Everyone receives a lot of emails and inboxes are loaded.

Not personalizing: Ever received an email with your name in the subject line? Or did you get an email from your vet containing your pet's name and favorite dog food along with a coupon? This is called personalization.

Not segmenting: Segmenting a list is simply the process of dividing it into sub-groups. While everyone on an email list may get some messages, you can then send extremely specific or targeted messages to just one group when the occasion arises. This lets you target individual readers who may be more receptive to your messages. Segmentation can have many benefits including the ability to target specific actions (buyers vs. non-buyers or openers vs. non-responders), or areas of interest (white wine vs. red or apartment rentals vs. houses for sale).

It is not visually appealing (okay, let us just say it... it is ugly): We are not usually this harsh, but man is there some ugly emails out there – anyone using Comic Sans font? And the sad thing is, they do not need to be ugly when there is a plethora of beautifully designed email templates out there just begging to be used. The good news is your email does not have to be ugly. With advances in email marketing, it is now drop-dead simple to create a great-looking email without a drop of graphic design experience.

Your email isn't responsive: When we say "isn't responsive" we don't mean your email is ignoring you, rather we are referring to the ability for your email to resize or reconfigure to the screen of the device the reader is using, whether it's a desktop, laptop, tablet, or smartphone. Why should you care?

Not delivering valuable content: Once a subscriber opens your email (because of your awesome subject line – #3), you've got just a few seconds to grab his or her attention. Stellar content can keep them engaged.

No call to action: Your call to action (CTA) should tell your reader exactly what you want them to do. So, make it obvious and use bold, action-oriented language in your CTAs. Tell your reader what you want them to do. We recommend using action verbs like Buy, Learn, Create, Start, Sign Up, etc.

You do not mail frequently enough, or you mail every day. single. day: A common question we get is "How often should I send emails out?" That is a tricky question in that there is no one-size-fits-all answer. What works for one business will not for another. A lot depends on your list, your product/service, and of course, what you promised your subscribers when they signed up. Your email sign-up form should very clearly articulate the benefit of joining your list and how often you will send emails. That helps manage expectations from the get-go.

Do not look at your reporting/analytics: You may be happily sending out your weekly newsletter and chugging along simply fine, but are you making the most of each of those newsletters? Your email reporting can help you decide. Reporting is not there to overwhelm you with a bunch of charts and graphs that do not mean anything. On the contrary, reports make it easy not only to see what is working but also make it clear what to do next.

Your email is anti-social: Every email service provides an effortless way to include icons and links to the social media sites your business has a presence on, so take advantage of this simple and effective way to allow your subscribers to connect with you in other ways. This is not the time to hide in the corner of the party. Get out there and get social with your subscribers.

You do not have goals: Another common mistake people make is sending emails without a clear idea of why they are sending them in the first place. We often hear, "I know I should be doing it, so I do." Ack! You need a better reason, and that reason can include any of the following: Helping your users and prospects, growing your list, driving visits to your physical location, website, or blog, generating revenue, booking appointments, or any or all these reasons. Email is an affordable and effective means of accomplishing all kinds of goals which is why is has continued to prosper for so long.

Chapter 14

Event Planning Checklist
<u>6 to 12 Months Ahead</u>

1. Decide event purpose (raise funds, visibility, celebration, etc.)
2. Choose a theme 3. Visit potential sites.
4. Research/select committees/chairpersons
5. Chairperson forms subcommittees
6. Get cost estimates (site rental, food, drinks, sound/lights, etc.)
7. Get recommendations for entertainment; hold auditions
8. Get bids for entertainment.
9. Get bids for decorations 10. Get bids for design/printing.
11. Get bids for other major items
12. Finance committee drafts initial budget
13. Create sponsorship amounts/levels.
14. List items to be underwritten and sources
15. Research/approach honorees.
16. Complete mailing list(individuals/businesses)
17. Check the proposed date for potential conflicts, and finalize date in writing
18. Get written contracts for site, entertainment, etc. 19. Develop alternative site (if event is outdoors)
20. Consider pre-party events for publicity or underwriting
21. Invite/confirm VIPs.
22. Pick graphic artist; begin invitation design
23. Order hold-the-date cards or other event announcements
24. Set marketing/public relations schedule

25.Develop press release and calendar listings 26. Select photographer; arrange for photos of VIPs, chairpersons, honorees.

27.Get biographical information on VIPs, celebrities, honorees, chairpersons

28.Investigate needs for special permits, licenses, insurance, etc.

<u>3-to-6-month Checklist</u>

1.Begin monthly committee meetings

2.Write/send requests for funding or underwriting to major donors, corporations, sponsors

3.Request logos from corporate sponsors for printing

4. Review graphic artist invitations, programs, posters, etc.

5.Prepare final copy for invitations, return card, posters

6. Prepare final copy for tickets.

7.Complete mailing list for invitations

8. Order invitations, posters, tickets, etc.

9. Sign contracts with entertainment company

10. Make a list of locations for posters

11. Finalize mailing lists; begin soliciting corporations and major donors

12. Obtain lists from honorees, VIPs

13. Obtain radio/TV sponsors, public service announcements, promos

14. Set menu with catering for food and beverages

15. Secure permits and insurance

16. Get written confirmation of celebrity participation, special needs

<u>4 weeks before the concert</u>

Place Posters in high-traffic areas such as Wal-Marts, Grocery Stores, laundry mats, and convenience stores.

Put an announcement about the concert on your venue's website.

<u>3 weeks before</u>

<u>concert</u> Offer flyers to post.

<u>2 weeks before the concert</u>

Send local radio stations press releases. Send press releases to the newspaper.

<u>1 Week before</u>

1. Meet with all committees for last-minute details

2. Finish phone follow-ups.

3. Confirm the number attending 4. Finish seating/table arrangements.

5. Hold training sessions with volunteers; finalize assignments

6. Secure two or three volunteers to assist with emergencies.

7.Finalize registration staff

8.Distribute seating chart assignments to hosts/hostesses

9. Schedule pickup or delivery of any rented or loaned equipment

10.Double-check arrival time and delivery times with vendors

11. Deliver final scripts/timelines to all program participants

12. Finalize catering guarantee, refreshments.

13.Confirm number of volunteers

14.Make follow-up calls to news media for advance and event coverage

15.Distribute additional fliers

16.Final walk-through with all personnel

17. Schedule volunteer assignments for day of event

18. Write checks for payments to be made for the day of the event.

<u>Day Before Event</u>

1.Recheck all equipment and supplies to be brought to the event.

<u>Event Day</u>

1.Arrive early (with your change of clothes

2.Unpack equipment, supplies, and make sure nothing is missing

3.Be sure all VIPs are in place and have scripts

4. Reconfirm refreshments/meal schedule for volunteers
5. Go over all the final details with caterer and setup staff
6. Check with volunteers to make sure all tasks are covered
7. Setup registration area
8.Check sound/light equipment and staging before rehearsal
9. Hold final rehearsal

Chapter 15

Advance the Date

Every band has had the experience at least once (and more than once) - you get to the venue, and no one is there to help you set up, the gear you need is nowhere to be found, and it seems like no one in town even knows you are playing. The way to avoid all this hassle is to advance your gig. Advancing your gig gives you an extra layer of insurance that everything will go smoothly on the night of the show, so all you must worry about is getting up there and playing a good set.

1. Assign the Task

"I thought you were going to do it." "No, you said you were." Sound like the kind of conversations you have with your bandmates in the run up to a gig. Advancing your gig is too important of a task to assume someone else is going to do. If your band has a manager or an agent, then the job of advancing the show will usually fall on their shoulders. If you have booked the show yourself, the job of advancing falls on someone in the band. It is a clever idea to have a band spokesperson who can act as the business contract for your band and take on responsibilities like these.

2. Promo On?

If you want people to come to your gig, you must promote it. Whose job depends on if you booked the gig with a promoter, who would take on most of these tasks, or if you are promoting the show yourself. If you are working with a promoter, it makes sense to check in during the run up to the show to make sure all promotional plans have been implemented. Ask questions like:

o Is the venue/town postered?

o Has the press been told about the gig?

o If there are to be ticket pre-sales, are the tickets ready and on sale?

Ideally, you should be looking at this stuff at least 4-6 weeks before the show.

3. Confirm the Details

Before the show, confirm the details in your contract, like:

o What time is load-in? Soundcheck? On stage time? Length of set?

o Will there be accommodation provided? Where? At whose cost?

o Will your rider or meal requests be, ok? o Have they arranged to meet all your tech needs? If you need special equipment, will they be able to provide it? At whose cost?

You should already know these answers, but it is funny how things change at the last minute. You should do this **1 week or so before the show** -late enough that final arrangements should be in

place, early enough to adapt if there are any problems.

4. The Final Day

On the day of your show, it is time for one last confirmation of the details. Check in with the promoter or venue early in the day to make sure everything is on track. If you had to make any changes to your original plan when you confirmed the details the first time, make sure those changes are all in place. Arrive on time for your load in/soundcheck and scope things out. If you see any problems with the stage set up, the gear, or anything else, speak up right away so you have the best chance of fixing things.

Tips:

1. Advancing your gig is a fantastic way to try and make things run a little more smoothly, but they are not a guarantee. Things can go wrong, things do go wrong - often, you can count on the fact that things WILL go wrong. Be ready to go with the flow - it will make things much easier for you. This is especially important for smaller, up-and-coming indie bands who may be working with smaller venues and part-time promoters. If something goes wrong, before becoming extremely angry, try to step back and weigh the situation. Trying to fix the problem and learning for next time is the best remedy for any show.

2. When you are confirming the details about things like hotel rooms and transportation with a promoter, it is worthwhile to triple-check by calling the hotel/the airline, etc., to see if they have a reservation for you.

3. Even if you are self-promoting a show, you can still advance the gig but running through the pre-gig checklist with yourself.

4. When you're confirming the details, that is also a good time to make sure you have directions to the venue and a contact number for someone in case you get lost coming into town (and you can bet you will - getting lost is part of being on tour).

5. While you are keeping everyone else on task, make sure you stay on yours. The one thing that is guaranteed to ruin a show is if you turn up not ready to play. You expect the promoters and venues to be professionals - make sure you are one, too.

Performance Info Needed.

Name of Gig Address Phone

Tech Supervisor Phone

Seating Capacity Date(s) of Gig How many dates How many times How many sets What times

Length of breaks

<u>Location Info Needed.</u>

House PA What kind
How many channels Board location House lights
What kind Rigging for lights Type
Console location Dimmer Spotlights Location
Sound and/or Light Tech Provided Any other crew members.
Type
How many Security Guards How many
Is stage elevated? How high
Corner or Flat wall Size of Stage Drum riser
Type of floor Dressing rooms Load in time What date Load out time.

What date

Load in location.

Accommodation Info Needed.

How many rooms Location

When can we arrive? Dates covered.

Any fees for accommodations Ample parking

Location Food Consisting of What times.

Payment for performance Who pays.

When is payment made? Check or Cash

Can we cash check @ venue?

Advertisement Info Needed.

List of Magazines and Newspapers (Press Release and Ads)

List of Radio (Send ID's, Promotions and Music) List of TV (Story Line)

Email List (Email Promotions)

List of Sponsors (Promotions and Ads) List of Charities (Coop with)

List of Convention Bureaus (Send Posters and Add Dates)

List of Record Stores (In Store Promotions) List of Cable TV (Coop Ads)

Posters and Flyers (Locations)

List of Organizations (Posters and Flyers) Invitations to Key People (Flyers and Promotions)

Key Promotions (Backstage Passes etc.)

Chapter 16

Market Your Business

Are you in a marketing rut? Are you ready to get[1] your business noticed [2]with a few easy-to-implement marketing ideas? Excellent, because we have a list of out-of-the-box ideas that will attract new customers and help to build buzz around your brand.

1. Online directories

The days of flipping through the Yellow Pages might be gone, but there are still many online directories your business can benefit from. These sites allow business owners to create a profile that offers information that their customers are most likely to search for including address, business hours, and pictures.

There are dozens of online directories [3]out there. Here are the top places to list your business:

Google Bing Yahoo Yelp

Yellow Pages White Pages Super pages yellow book

---

1. http://www.verticalresponse.com/blog/facebook-boosted-posts-3-ways-to-target-your-audience/

2. http://www.verticalresponse.com/blog/facebook-boosted-posts-3-ways-to-target-your-audience/

3. http://www.verticalresponse.com/blog/top-20-places-business-needs-listed-online/

Manta

City Search MapQuest Foursquare

The Business Journals Angie's List

Hot Frog

IS YOUR BUSINESS ALREADY listed online? Deluxe Corporation offers a free online directory search[4] tool [5]that you can use to check the status of your company across the most popular online directories and ensure all the information listed is correct.

2. Review sites

Wor[6]d of mouth [7]is still one of the best ways to market your business. These days you can also encourage word-of-mouth marketing for your business online through review sites.[8]

Like online directories, there are many to choose from. Some of the most influential include:

- **Yelp**[9]. A popular option for restaurants and brick-and-mortar shops.

---

4. https://ww.deluxe.com/small-business/search-engine-marketing/online-directory-scan

5. https://ww.deluxe.com/small-business/search-engine-marketing/online-directory-scan

6.   http://www.verticalresponse.com/blog/3-highly-effective-word-of-mouth-marketing-tactics/

7.   http://www.verticalresponse.com/blog/3-highly-effective-word-of-mouth-marketing-tactics/

8.   http://www.virgin.com/entrepreneur/10-reasons-customer-reviews

9. http://www.yelp.com/

- **Googl**[10]**e My Busi**[11]**ness**[12]. A great option for both brick-and-mortar businesses and e-commerce businesses. (You can get more

---

10. https://www.google.com/business/

11. https://www.google.com/business/

12. https://www.google.com/business/

information about this tool in a previous[13] VerticalResponse post.[14])

• **Angie's List[15]**. A useful review platform used for service-based businesses.

3. Beneficial online marketing tools

There are a few specific tools that small business owners should explore when thinking about ways to boost their marketing efforts. Here are four of our favorites:

• **Full [16]C[17]ontact[18]**

Good marketing and practical networking often go hand in hand. The next time you attend an industry trade show, [19]an event at your local Chamber of Commerce, or even a simple social gathering, make sure you have Full Contact on your smartphone. With this app, you can snap a picture of a business card, and the contact[20] information is automatically loaded [21]into your VerticalResponse contact list.

• **Just[22]uno[23]**

13. http://www.verticalresponse.com/blog/whats-all-the-buzz-about-google-my-business/

14. http://www.verticalresponse.com/blog/whats-all-the-buzz-about-google-my-business/

15. http://www.angieslist.com

16. http://www.verticalresponse.com/integrations/fullcontact

17. http://www.verticalresponse.com/integrations/fullcontact

18. http://www.verticalresponse.com/integrations/fullcontact

19. http://www.verticalresponse.com/blog/3-ways-break-noise-trade-show/

20. http://techcrunch.com/2014/12/16/fullcontact-for-gmail-is-the-latest-email-plugin-to-take-on-linkedins-rapportive/

21. http://techcrunch.com/2014/12/16/fullcontact-for-gmail-is-the-latest-email-plugin-to-take-on-linkedins-rapportive/

Effective marketing also requires that you work[24] hard to grab the attentio[25]n of you[26]r audience[27]. With Justuno, you can do just that. This handy widget allows you to add an instant offer/promo to your website or social sites. Before getting the offer, the visitor must submit his or her email address.

---

22. http://www.verticalresponse.com/integrations/justuno

23. http://www.verticalresponse.com/integrations/justuno

24.   http://www.verticalresponse.com/blog/a-5-step-recipe-to-snag-subscribers-attention/

25.   http://www.verticalresponse.com/blog/a-5-step-recipe-to-snag-subscribers-attention/

26.   http://www.verticalresponse.com/blog/a-5-step-recipe-to-snag-subscribers-attention/

27.   http://www.verticalresponse.com/blog/a-5-step-recipe-to-snag-subscribers-attention/

This comprehensive tool gets people talking about your business and adds them to your contact list.

- **Pr[28]ez[29]ly[30]**

When something newsworthy happens with your business, always consider cre[31]ating a press release[32] to share with the media. In addition to emailing, it to your local TV stations and newspapers, you should also share it on Prezly.com. This site places your press releases in front of leading digital newsrooms and other social media[33] influencers[34].

- **Fou[35]rs[36]quare[37]**

Boost your overall social media presence with Foursquare. When someone visits your business, they can "check in" on Foursquare[38], which tells their social media audience where the user is. Your business name will then show up in their social network news feeds, which is perfect free publicity without any upfront effort.

---

28. https://www.prezly.com

29. https://www.prezly.com

30. https://www.prezly.com

31.   http://www.verticalresponse.com/blog/page/3/?s=press+release

32.   http://www.verticalresponse.com/blog/page/3/?s=press+release

33.   http://www.adweek.com/socialtimes/marketers-struggle-to-identify-and-engage-social-media-influencers-report/622991

34.   http://www.adweek.com/socialtimes/marketers-struggle-to-identify-and-engage-social-media-influencers-report/622991

35. https://foursquare.com

36. https://foursquare.com

37. https://foursquare.com

38.   http://www.verticalresponse.com/blog/the-newest-location-based-social-apps-cool-or-creepy/

4. Offline marketing ideas

Remember though, despite the push to be everywhere online, offline marketing still has its place. Here are a few ideas to consider when looking to take your business marketing off the digital grid:

• Join a local business group.

Join a local business group like the Chamber of[39] Commerce [40]or other business-oriented groups. These organizations will usually host social gatherings, distribute newsletters, and participate in volunteer events, all of which are opportunities to market your business.

• Keep 'marketing swag' in hand.

From pens to T-shirts and everything in between, it is important to get (and work to keep!) Your name out there. Make sure that you have a stocked inventory of marketing swag goodies[41] available at all times whether you own a physical or online business. In addition to wearing, it yourself, set aside an amount to give away to customers each month as well.

More Ways to Promote Your Small Business for Free

One of the best things about living in the online era is that we get access to so many wonderful tools to promote our businesses! We are spoilt for choice! Some small actions and some big.

Choose a few that will reach your target market with the message you want to send. Then see how it goes, re-evaluate, and try again!

---

39.   https://www.uschamber.com/

40.   https://www.uschamber.com/

41.   http://www.google.com/
url?sa=t&rct=j&q=&esrc=s&source=web&cd=9&ved=0CF4QFjAI&url=http%3A%2F%
2Fprincetonmarketing.net%2Fprincetonmarketingblog%2Fmarketing%2Fhow-much-
brand%25E2%2580%2593building-power-does-promotional-swag-
carry&ei=KRmcVe2FJNjfoASb45KgBg&usg=AFQjCNH94pnZcwGT4dxG4qlCON0otE
b84g&bvm=bv.96952980,d.cGU

One common goal for it is simply to increase your search ranking in Google. Plus, it also gives you something great to share on social media or to entice someone to sign up to your email list (call to action).

1. Create a Blog Post that Teaches the Beginning of Something

2. Create a Blog Post that Supplements your Product or Service

3. Create a Portfolio

4. Create a "Challenge."

5. Create a Free E-book, Checklist or Workbook 6. Create an Infographic

7. Create a YouTube Video 8. Create a Quiz

9. Create a SlideShare

10. Create a Webinar or Online Workshop 11. Write a Vanity/ Roundup Post

12. Link, Link, Link!!

13. Repurpose, Repurpose, Repurpose!!

14. Add social media Sharing Buttons to your Website

15. Use a Consistent Profile Picture and Image Style

16. Create specific Images for your Promotions to share on all your chosen Platforms

17. Share, Share, Share your Content!!

18. Create a Great Facebook Cover Photo and Twitter Header Image

19. Put your "Business Page" as your workplace on your Personal Facebook Profile

20. Create a More Memorable Bio Description 21. Add a Link to your Opt-In or Great Piece of info in all your bios.

22. Create a "Pinned" Post for your Facebook and Twitter Pages

23. Create a Google+ Profile

Anything to help your Google Rankings! 24. Strategically use Hashtags

25. Join Pinterest Group Boards and Post to Those

26. Do a Periscope or Facebook Live Video 27. "Retweet" or share great content from supplementary businesses or bloggers (and tag them when you do!)

28. Share images on Instagram or Facebook that support your Brand Personality

29. Schedule Online Q&A Times/Office Hours (via FB, Twitter, Periscope)

30. Write a Blog Post for LinkedIn

31. Customize your signature in your Normal Emails

32. Follow up new subscribers with some other content they might be interested in

33. Author Emails that Contain something they Cannot see Anywhere else

34. Send out Promotions (but not too often!)

35. Follow up with People who JUST purchased with a how to use the product or other relevant additional information.

36. Follow up with People who purchased requesting feedback and offer extra advice

37. Create a free E-mail Course as your Content Opt-In

38. Find a list of potential customers and send them PERSONALISED one on one emails with a conversational message

39. Participate in Facebook Groups 40. Join in Twitter Chats

41. Comment on Other Blogs or Videos

42. Reply to Comments on Competitors Blogs 43. Participate in Online Forums

44. Ask your Friends and Family to Spread the Word

45. Ask for a Product or Service Review from Influencers

46. Guest Post on a Successful Blog for your industry

47. Ask to be Interviewed on a Podcast 48. Make a Coffee Date!

49. Offer to Speak at Events or Workshops where your Target Customer is in the Audience

50. Apply for Business Awards

51. Get a Magnetic Sign made up for Your Car

Chapter 17

Marketing You and Your Music

1. You have a great looking, fast loading, up-to-date interactive website that is separate from all your social network sites. It has your name as the URL (e.g., www.myband.com).

2. You are steadily building a larger and larger fan base.

3. You encourage and entice everyone to sign up for your email list and you get their first names, email addresses and zip codes.

4. You send an interesting, funny, interactive newsletter at least once a month that includes a call to action (e.g., vote for your favorite song on my CD and get a free download). 5. You only have an active social network presence on those key websites that are most relevant to your act.

6. You interact with your fans on a one-on-one and small group basis to build real relationships with them, resulting in their desire to buy your music and merchandise.

7. You have a brand statement that describes your act in one short phrase or sentence, and it is highly visible everywhere your name is.

8. You use free downloads, free merchandise, and other enticements to engage your fans.

9. Everything you do has the end purpose of subtly leading your fans to where they can buy your music.

10. You appreciate your fans and let them know about it on your website and in your newsletters and reward them for their loyalty.

MARKETING TIPS

1. Make stickers of URL and plaster them everywhere. 2. Email all your friends of the website

3. Put your website on merchandise

4. Give away things at gigs with your web site on them

5. Sell space in your CD booklet using pictures of the advertisers

Marketing words

1. You – Write as though you're speaking to the customer and about the customer, not about yourself.

2. Because – Give customers a reason they need to act.

3. Free – "Because" we all like free things, right?

4. Value – This implies customers are getting something versus losing something (i.e., money when you say "cost" or "price").

5. Guaranteed – Give customers a guarantee to minimize risk perception, so they feel they have everything to gain and nothing to lose.

6. Amazing – Customers will respond to something that is incredible.

7. Easy – Make it simple for customers to take the next step in the purchasing process and let them know how much easier life will be with your product or service.

8. Discover – This implies there is something new and unknown to the customer, something that has supreme benefits and gives them an edge.

9. Act now – Motivate an immediate response with a limited-time offer.

10. Everything included/everything you need – This establishes that your product or service is all your customers will have to buy to achieve their goal.

11. Never – Point out a "negative benefit," such as "never worry again" or "never overpay again."

12. New – Your product or service is the forefront in your industry.

13. Save – The most powerful word to showcase monetary savings, or even time savings.

14. Proven – Remind customers that your product, service, or business is tried-and-true.

15. Safe and effective – "Proven" to minimize risk perception for health and monetary loss.

16. Powerful – Let customers know that your business, product, or service is robust.

17. Actual results/guaranteed results – Your customers want results.

18. Secret – Not everyone succeeds, and there are secrets to success. Let customers know you can reveal those secrets.

19. The – This implies your solution is the "end-all-be-all." Consider the difference: "3 Solutions for Marketing Success"/" The 3 Solutions for Marketing Success."

20. Instant –Instant access or downloads are more appealing than waiting.

21. How to – Start off with a solution so customers read the rest of your copy.

22. Elite –Your customers are among the best in the world. Invite newbies to join a highly desirable club.

23. Premium – Premium helps denote high quality.

24. Caused by – If your marketing literature builds a case for your product, transitional phrases such as "caused by," "therefore," and "thus" can help reinforce the logic of a purchase.

25. More – Do you offer more than your competitors? Let your customers know because they want the best deal.

26. Bargain – Because customers want a great deal, remember?

27. No obligation – Create a win-win situation for your customers.

28. 100% money-back guarantee – Again, no risk.

29. Huge – A large discount or outstanding offer is difficult to resist.

30. Wealth – If you are selling products and services related to money, wealth is a desirable word for customers.

The key to success is to combine these words into phrases that trigger buying behavior. For example: "Get real results instantly – 100% money-back guarantee – act now!" Keep your copy brief, play on emotional triggers with these words and phrases, and you will increase your conversion and response rates.

Market your new services

This advice is nothing new, but with most of the planet glued to their screens, there is no better time to leverage social media and get your business out there. Do Instagram Live sessions, Facebook Live shows, YouTube tutorials, and TikTok videos. On each one, let your audience know they can book you for virtual events!

You are a busy person! You do not have time to pour hours and hours into having an amazing social media presence across multiple platforms, and that is okay! Instead of having a mediocre presence on Facebook, Twitter, Instagram, Tumblr, LinkedIn, and Pinterest, it is better to have a strong presence on one or two of these platforms. Choose the social network(s) that suit your business the best and encourage the most interaction from fans and clients. For example, if you are a photographer, you might opt for Facebook and Instagram. But comedians may have a better experience on Twitter. Regardless of what you do, it is wise to use LinkedIn to network and connect with past, present, and future clients.

Chapter 18

Quickly Jumpstart Your Marketing Efforts

A newspaper reporter recently interviewed me for a business column on marketing and asked what I thought was a great question:

How can a company that stopped or cut back on its marketing during the recession regain marketing momentum?

Here is one thing you can do right away whether you are a company or an individual, and whether you have cut back on marketing, or you are just getting started.

While the best methods for jumpstarting a marketing campaign can vary depending on the industry, in general, the first thing I would do is immediately pull together a database of past, current and prospective customers and start communicating with them. If you are just getting started, create a database of all the people you know who might be interested in hearing from you. That includes friends, family members, former business associates - everyone.

Start communicating with them, not by trying to sell your product, service, or book, but by providing valuable information. If you are a businessperson or professional, it should address topics relevant to the problems that you solve. Authors might share information relevant to their work or the issues and themes they address in their book. A physician, for instance, can share tips for staying healthy; a financial professional might offer retirement advice; someone with a beauty product can write about ways to look younger, and a mystery writer can share behind-the-scenes insights.

Create a newsletter, tip of the day or some other format that works for you. Establish a schedule for distributing it via email and then send it out like clockwork. Consistency is important.

By providing your recipients with useful, helpful information, you demonstrate your expertise in your field while building a trusting relationship. Your newsletter will remind your past customers of all you have to offer, and they will be your best prospects for recent sales. It will strengthen the confidence your current customers have in you, and it will encourage prospective customers to move toward a sale.

But do not stop there!

You need to keep that database of contacts growing, so you will want to establish other means for doing that. On your website, you can offer free reports available as downloads when people sign up for them. You can offer how-to videos or free subscriptions to your blog or newsletter so people can have them delivered automatically. If you are an author, how about providing a chapter of your book?

With everything you do, your goal will be to entice people to visit your website so they can connect with you and be added to your marketing database. What are some other ways to get them there?

* **Traditional media:** Share your useful information with radio, TV and print audiences - newspapers and magazines as well as online news sites - to get more visibility for your name, business, and website. This kind of publicity not only gets you more exposure, but it also gives you credibility no amount of advertising can buy. When talk show hosts and journalists turn to you as an authoritative source of information, they give you their implied endorsement.

* **Social media:** If you are not using social media, you need to start! Here again, you will use social networking sites such as Twitter, LinkedIn and/or Google+ to share valuable information relevant to your business or book. Your goal is to build followers on each platform who are interested in your message and may become prospective clients or customers.

But while developing connections on social media is important, remember, the overriding purpose is to grow your marketing database. You can do this by offering your followers opportunities to visit your website by occasionally posting links to new material there, such as photos or a blog post.

* **Other ways to address audiences:** There are many ways to get in front of people. They include speaking engagements -start locally by speaking to church and civic groups, clubs, and the chamber of commerce. You can offer to speak at seminars or host your own. Sponsor a charitable event or launch your own blog talk radio show.

Marketing is the life blood of every business, no matter what you are selling. When you stop or slow your marketing efforts, you will eventually see the consequences for your sales. It may take time to build traction but be patient and work away at it.

Help people by giving them information they can use, and you will not only keep your customer database growing with new names,

but you will also maintain and strengthen existing relationships. And
- this is the nice part - you will enjoy it.

Chapter 19

Another Attitude Another Way

The story begins online, just like it used to begin in clubs. Sure, you need music. But that is just the kindling to start a fire online.

Have you ever built a fire? If you load up the big logs first, it does not take. You must start with exceedingly small twigs. You've. to nurture the flame, blowing air on it or gently using bellows. Then you lay on increasingly large pieces, not getting to logs until you are just shy of a conflagration. That is how you build careers today.

1. Focus on the music. You need at most four songs. Anymore and confuse the audience. Less is okay, but you want to encourage a story, you do not want to appear a one-hit-wonder.

2. As you gain traction, you put out more music. You do not worry about selling the original music to everybody on the planet, at this point, you only focus on your core.

3. You make the music available. Do not try to monetize it at first, that just slows down the process of building your career. People can hear it streamed online, and they can download it and trade it.

4. Interact online, and do not talk to your fans. Do not tell them you are the next big star. Hi. op bluster is passe. Be thrilled that they are interested in you and your music. Tell them everything they want to know, and more. Put up pictures of your girl or boyfriend. Tell them what you do every day. If you have a family, do not hide it, reveal it. Your goal is to humanize yourself. Artifice is so seventies. The Net community is about using out the truth. Give them the truth and your honesty will endear you to them.

5. Do not ask your fans to spread the word. Do not ask them to be street-teamers. Do not have a street team! If they like your music and you treat them well, they will spread the word just like a kid telling his mother about his new best friend. They will not be able to hold back. There is no money in it for the fan. So let him retain his dignity. Let him believe he is your best friend.

6. Do not alert the mainstream media. That comes last. Once you have built something, once you have a story. Like Dispatch playing Madison Square Garden. If your story is not interesting to those who do not care, do not tell it, or sell it. As I said, I am not interested in vampire books, but the phenomenon intrigued me.

This is ass-backwards to the way it has been. In recent scenarios, music has come last. It was about image. It was about marketing. So, there is no traction, no connection with the consumer/fan. With looks being everything, "artists" have become models. Pretty faces with no depth. And you wonder why the "Hills" stars are more famous than most musicians... Because musicians do not have that something extra, the music that sets them apart!

You are building a party, a club. You do not want to let everyone in, you do not want everyone to come. When the nerds are partying, they do not want the athletes crashing, with their beer and belligerence. You are building a community of nerds. Nerds will build your band. If you are not interested in nerds. You had better be Christina Aguilera, with a big voice and Top Forty airplay. Nerds need music to get by. They do not have enough of a social life. Their life is online. Nerds come first, then the popular kids, then the public. You want people with plenty of time to sit online and spread the word. Kids who know the ins and outs of the Web. This is your audience. Do not play to the last row, do not play to people who do not care. Chances are you are a nerd too if you would only admit it to yourself... You are playing music because you have trouble talking or meeting a different sex. Your online nerd base wants to embrace you... LET THEM!

And if you are good, the casual user will find out about

you and your music overall. Because mainstream media NEEDS a story, and you will have one. But since the publicity does not come overnight... Since you drove across the country, stopping in shopping malls and bars before you rocketed to the moon, your original fans will not abandon you, because they have invested time, and they have knowledge no casual fan can have. They are bonded, they are dedicated. They will keep you alive after your mainstream fame has dried up. But they will not stay with you if you switch allegiance to all those people the nerds decry, in quick order.

But it all comes down to creating something people like. And what people like most is not slick, not glossy, over-produced songs written by guns-for-hire, but straight from the heart original numbers. You do not have to create a new genre. But you do have to be good. Hell, just like Stephenie Meyer, notice a tried-and-true genre and give it your twist. Siblings can be the new Carpenters. Scruffy kids can be the new Beatles. Do not waste a lot of time for no reason unless you have that ability. Clive Davis is right in one regard; you must have your hit. A hit is something irresistible, not a track that is driven to the top of the chart by big company money. Create your hit, and you will get a fan base. But, from there, know that you are the leader of the gang. But the gang is more like a Boy Scout troop or a group of Brownies. But Boy Scouts and Brownies desire to break through into adulthood. You are going to help them, by giving them the tools to show the rest of the world that not only do they matter, but they are also aligned with the best stuff out there, and they have been dedicated from the very beginning!

Chapter 20

Virtual Shows

VIRTUAL SERVICES ARE not a new concept, but they are certainly a growing trend amidst the stay-at-home orders and restrictions on public events. Many performers and entertainers are finding virtual events to be a wonderful way to make up for lost gigs during this lull in the economy. Offering virtual services is a terrific addition to your business, but it is important to learn all you can about making them successful.

BEFORE THE GIG

AS WITH ANY GIG, PREPARATION is important. Since you are relying so much on technology, a virtual event may need even more attention to make sure things run smoothly.

KNOW THE PLATFORMS.

THERE ARE LOTS OF PLATFORMS you can choose from, but we will discuss the most popular choices below. These are likely to be most well-known to your clients, too, which will make things easier for both of you.

ZOOM

AS A FREE CONFERENCING software, Zoom has risen above the competition. While it does have a 40-minute time limit on its free service, that is usually plenty of time for a virtual event. You can record the calls and share them later if you would like. It also allows for customizable backgrounds, which can be fun! But most importantly, it boasts HD video and audio.

HOWEVER, IF YOU ARE a musician, you may have trouble with its features that are aimed toward video conferencing – meaning it attempts to block out noise such as music. This option may be best for virtual events looking for character visits, birthday telegrams, or motivational speakers.

LASTLY, ZOOM ALLOWS you to see up to forty-nine participants at once (100 total) which makes it ideal for virtual events with large groups.

FACEBOOK LIVE

ANOTHER FREE AND WELL-known option is Facebook Live. Participants can join the Facebook Live call via link, even if they do not have a Facebook account. You will not be able to make this private, so keep that in mind if it is of concern to you or your client.

Skype

AS ONE OF THE FIRST services to offer video conferences, most people are familiar with this platform. While it does lack some of the features of Zoom, it is extremely easy to set up Skype will store your recorded meetings for up to 30 days, which allows you and your client to download and save it if you would like. If you (or your client) find it complicated to download new software, you might consider Skype Meet Now which allows participants to join with a click – no new applications are necessary.

Check your equipment.

WHEN PREPARING TO DELVE into the world of virtual events, you should take a moment to check over your audio and visual equipment. We have all experienced the frustration of a choppy online meeting, and you certainly do not want a paying client to have that same annoyance.

MAKE SURE YOUR AUDIO quality is possible.

What your camera/video equipment picks up is sometimes wildly different from what you hear, so it is important to have someone else listen to the product, so you know how to adjust. You must know ahead of time how to compensate and how to set your levels."

Create your space.

SETTING UP YOUR BACKGROUND or your set is an important consideration when you are participating in a virtual event. You do not want to appear unprofessional by sitting on your unmade bed while you deliver a singing telegram or reading a fairy tale with a pile of dirty dishes behind you.

THE MAIN THING IS TO be sure your space is clean and free of clutter. "A blank wall works well. I have a plain interior brick wall that I use, and my clients have appreciated it," says Celeste Vee. "I have had one who requested a cool virtual background and that's easy to do on Zoom."

PERFORMING ON CAMERA can be a bit different than your live show, so think about how to set your camera angle. Play around with different distances, lenses, and angles to find one that best fits your performance. It is all about finding the right compromise between allowing them to see facial expressions and still giving yourself room to move and entertain."

Practice, practice, practice.

IF IT IS NOT CLEAR by now, virtual events are much different than live events and can come with a multitude of unexpected issues. While you may still have some glitches, spend some time ironing those out ahead of time. Set everything up the exact way you would for your event, then recruit a friend or family member to be your audience. Try asking the following questions to get some valuable feedback on your virtual performance:

JUST BECAUSE YOU HAVE done a Facebook Live show does not mean it will translate to Zoom. You may have called your mom on FaceTime hundreds of times, but you may not know how to successfully pull off a Skype event. Do not wait until the day of the show – give yourself lots of time to get the kinks worked out! There is no such thing as too much practice.

DURING THE GIG

THE BIG MOMENT HAS finally arrived! When you are ready to begin your virtual performance, we have a few more tips to make sure things go smoothly.

AVOID INTERRUPTIONS.

WHEN WE GO TO THE MOVIE theater, the first thing we are told is to turn off our electronic devices. Be sure to apply the same principle to your virtual events! Being at home means you have lots of distractions around you but take some time to remove them.

If you have pets, roommates, or children, have them go to a different room while you perform. Put a note on your doorbell asking delivery people to avoid ringing it. If you are using a computer, make sure it (and other necessary devices) is fully charged or plugged into a power source.

LASTLY, SWITCH YOUR devices to do-not-disturb mode. Celeste Vee shares her cringe-worthy moment when she forgot to turn her phone to airplane mode: "I was in the middle of a virtual gig and a friend tried to FaceTime me. Since I was performing along with a track running on my Mac, it interrupted the performance completely and the music stopped. So amateur and embarrassing!"

MAKE THE CALL.

ONE OF THE FREQUENT questions we get about virtual events is "Who calls who?" We suggest that you work with your client to decide on who starts the call during an online performance. The artist should be the one to initiate the call, so they take control of the event from the beginning. Even though virtual events may be a new-ish concept to performers and clients alike, your clients are still looking to you for guidance. Santa Ed says, "I always call them. This allows me to be 100% ready for the call."

KEEP CLIENTS ENGAGED.

SOMETIMES THE SCREEN does not translate as well as an in-person event does. This may require you to change things up a bit for your virtual performances. Being a captivating performer is always important, but here are some tips for keeping your on-screen clients engaged.

MUSICIANS AND SINGERS

YOU MIGHT BE USED TO playing several full-length songs with a few breaks in between, but that may not work as well with virtual events. Keep your songs short; I usually keep them around 2-3 minutes each. You rarely need to perform an entire song. Be sure to eliminate awkward gaps in between. We are event entertainers so we do not usually talk much between songs, and your performances should be seamless from song to song. This is extremely popular with virtual clients, and they always compliment them on how keeping their attention is important.

KEEPING YOUR ENERGY up is also important since you are the sole focus of the event. Having a screen between you and your audience can put up a barrier to the vibe that is usually created with live music. Help break it down with lots of smiles and positive energy. Medleys or shorter versions of songs are fine, and practice and preparation are crucial.

Visual artists

ARTISTS WHO OFFER SERVICES like dancing, magic, or puppetry may have an easier time transitioning to virtual events. It is a bit like watching TV for your audience, so if you are doing something interesting, they will be entertained! It is not as easy to keep their attention as you might with a live event, so consider trimming your performance or sets to move things along a bit faster. Give them small bites of entertainment rather than a long performance that may cause your audience to drift.

TALK TO THE CAMERA. If there are kids, ask them to respond. Use visual aids and move closer to the camera at times." Tony also prefers to record his performance ahead of time so he can re-use it for several events and have more control over the recording. To keep things interesting, he suggests "Have your camera person push 'pause' and change the distance or angle."

Characters and impersonators

ASK QUESTIONS! IF YOU are doing a live chat with a child (or adult) and want to keep them engaged, it is important to have some questions ahead of time. You might dig in a bit with the event planner and learn about the guest of honor's favorite movies, hobbies, food, and more.

SET THE RIGHT PRICE.

ONE OF THE BENEFITS of a virtual gig is that you do not have to go anywhere. Most of our vendors have elected to offer lower pricing for virtual events because they have cut down on travel costs and setup time. While this may mean you have to do more virtual events than live events, this option can still help performers get through the lull in the industry.

TO FIGURE OUT YOUR own pricing, we would suggest charging the cost of 1 hour of your normal rate. Most virtual events are not close to an hour long, but it still covers the time you will need to set up, rehearse, and prepare for the event. Without having to travel, you should hopefully be making a fair amount for each booking.

DO NOT CHARGE AS MUCH for virtual events. For live events, I spend a lot of time driving to the gig, loading in, setting up my equipment, tearing down, loading out and driving home. Now I just put on my makeup, walk into my studio, and perform! I cannot personally justify charging the same for a 30-minute show as I would for an entire evening."

PROMOTE YOUR SERVICES.

VIRTUAL EVENTS ARE the growing trend right now, so it is crucial that you market yourself as someone who offers virtual services. Check out the following posts to get started with your marketing efforts:

Your past clients are another major source of marketing. They may be looking for ways to shake up corporate meetings or did not know they could still celebrate their kiddo's birthday on-screen. Reach out to your previous bookings and let them know about your new flexible service options!

IF YOU HAVE CLIENTS who need to postpone or have asked to cancel their bookings, you might take the opportunity to offer a virtual alternative to canceling completely.

Chapter 21

How to make money with music online[1]

NOTHING ELSE IN HISTORY has shaped the music industry more dramatically than the internet. But as much as it is played an integral role in countless musicians' careers, the coronavirus crisis has now put us in a position where, for the first time ever, the internet is our only option to reach music fans.

THE UNFORTUNATE REALITY we have to face is that it could be a quite a while [2]before live performances, tours, and festivals will be back in full swing. If gigging has made up a good chunk of your income up until this point, it is crucial that you start laying the groundwork now to make money from your music [3]online.

THE GOOD NEWS IS THAT once we come out on the other side of this pandemic, all the effort you put in now to supplement your income will continue to pay off over time. So how can you make

---

1. **https://bandzoogle.com/blog/how-to-make-money-with-music-online**

2. https://consequenceofsound.net/2020/04/health-expert-concerts-wont-return-fall-2021/

3. https://bandzoogle.com/blog/18-ways-musicians-can-make-money

money with music online? Here are some of the best ways to get started. 1. Sell music through your website

If you don't already have one, you should build a[4] website for your music[5]. It gives you a little slice of the internet that you own and control, and you can also sell[6] music directly to your fans [7](commission-free through Bandzoogle).

BUT MORE THAN THAT, you will own the data and emails you collect through it. This is essential to have long-term success in your career, as you can use that data to let your fans know about contemporary music, upcoming tours, crowdfunding campaigns, and more.

CHECK OUT: The complete guide to selling your music[8] online[9]

2. Make your music available through online music retailers

Fans don't buy as many digital downloads as they used[10] to, [11]but they can still be a meaningful revenue source for DIY musicians.

Distributing your music [12]to major online retailers like iTunes and Amazon helps you come across as a more legitimate artist, gives

---

4. https://bandzoogle.com/blog/how-to-make-a-website-for-your-music

5. https://bandzoogle.com/blog/how-to-make-a-website-for-your-music

6. https://bandzoogle.com/features/sell-music

7. https://bandzoogle.com/features/sell-music

8. https://bandzoogle.com/blog/the-complete-guide-to-selling-your-music-online

9. https://bandzoogle.com/blog/the-complete-guide-to-selling-your-music-online

10. https://musically.com/2019/09/06/us-recorded-music-business-grew-by-18-in-first-half-of-2019/

11. https://musically.com/2019/09/06/us-recorded-music-business-grew-by-18-in-first-half-of-2019/

you access to detailed analytics, and gives your fans a convenient way to support you.

3. Make your music available for streaming

These days, most of the listening is happening on major streaming platforms like Spotify, Apple Music, Google Play, and Amazon Music. This means that making your songs available on them is essential to reach your current fans, as well as potential new fans.

WE HAVE A LONG WAY to go before streaming revenue replaces the money that artists used to make selling physical albums, but the business is growing every year[13], and it's income you don't want to miss out on collecting.

ONCE YOU DISTRIBUTE your music to these platforms, you can boost your stream count with tactics like pre-save[14] campaigns[15], audio ads[16], and playlist features[17].

4. Monetize your YouTube channel

How can a hardworking musician get their hands on some of that sweet, sweet YouTube money? The first and easiest step is to

---

12.   https://cdbaby.com/digital-distribution

13. https://www.theverge.com/2020/2/26/21154504/riaa-report-paid-subscriptions-93-percent-streaming-revenue-growth-2019

14. https://diymusician.cdbaby.com/music-promotion/boost-streams-pre-save-campaign-spotify/

15. https://diymusician.cdbaby.com/music-promotion/boost-streams-pre-save-campaign-spotify/

16. https://diymusician.cdbaby.com/music-promotion/how-to-create-an-effective-spotify-audio-ad-for-your-music/

17. https://bandzoogle.com/blog/how-to-get-your-music-featured-on-spotify-playlists

upload all your music to your channel. From there, you need to build up your[18] subscribers [19]and set up YouTube monetization [20]on your account.

ANYTIME MUSIC YOU OWN is used in a YouTube video — whether on your own channel or someone else's

— you're entitled to collect your fair share [21]of the ad revenue generated by it. A digital distribution company such as CD Baby [22]will help ensure that all the money you're owed ends up in your bank account.

5. Finance your next project through crowdfunding

If you have a supportive fanbase, crowdfunding can be a wonderful way to cover the costs of your project. The key to successful crowdfunding is to build excitement among your most engaged fans [23]by showing them what's behind the curtain and inviting them into your creative

process. It takes a lot of planning and proper budgeting[24],

---

18.   https://diymusician.cdbaby.com/youtube/how-to-increase-your-youtube-subscribers-with-one-simple-link/

19.   https://diymusician.cdbaby.com/youtube/how-to-increase-your-youtube-subscribers-with-one-simple-link/

20.   https://support.google.com/youtube/answer/72857?hl=en

21.   https://diymusician.cdbaby.com/youtube/youtube-musicians-made/

22.   https://cdbaby.com/youtube.aspx

23.   https://bandzoogle.com/blog/how-to-engage-your-community-around-a-crowdfunding-campaign

24.   https://bandzoogle.com/blog/crowdfunding-your-album-11-dos-don-ts

though, so do not think of it as a quick fix that will solve your immediate cash flow problems.

WHEN YOU'RE READY TO launch your campaign, you can use Bandzoogle's built-in crowdfunding tools [25] to take album pre-orders, bundle digital music with CDs or vinyl, and anything else you'd like to offer. Unlike other crowdfunding platforms, pledges from your fans are commission-free on Bandzoogle and go directly into your account with no delays.

SELL MUSIC, MERCH, and tickets, take direct donations, pledges for crowdfunding, and create monthly fan subscriptions from your website, all commission-free. Try Bandzoogle free for 30 days to build a website [26] for your music. [27]

6. Offer fan subscriptions

One of the hardest things about making a living as a musician is that most income streams are unpredictable. Fan subscriptions have emerged as one of the few reliable sources of recurring revenue, making it an especially attractive option for artists in such uncertain times.

SUBSCRIPTIONS (SOMETIMES referred to as memberships) give your most loyal fans access to exclusive recordings, performances, videos, merch, and rewards in exchange for a small monthly contribution.

---

25. https://bandzoogle.com/features/crowdfunding

26. https://bandzoogle.com/

27. https://bandzoogle.com/

IT TAKES A LOT OF EFFORT and dedication to consistently churn out new content and creative ideas for rewards[28], but if you're up for that sort of challenge, it's an excellent way to form deeper relationships with your listeners.

BANDZOOGLE MEMBERS have access to a built-

in subscriptions feature [29]that makes all of this super easy to set up. Best of all, the monthly income that you earn is commission-free and gets paid directly to you.

LEARN MORE: How to sell fan subscriptions on your[30] music website[31]

7. Sell tickets to live stream shows

With venues shut down around the world, music fans are more willing than ever to support artists online right now. Selling access to exclusive live streams [32]of your performances can help you make money without having to leave home.

EXPERIMENT WITH DEBUTING new material, playing through a beloved album in its entirety, and even taking audience requests to get a better sense of what your fans want to hear.

---

28. https://bandzoogle.com/blog/71-ways-to-reward-your-music-fan-subscribers

29.   https://bandzoogle.com/features/subscriptions

30. https://bandzoogle.com/blog/how-to-sell-fan-subscriptions-on-your-music-website

31. https://bandzoogle.com/blog/how-to-sell-fan-subscriptions-on-your-music-website

32.   https://bandzoogle.com/blog/new-sell-tickets-to-live-streams

LEARN MORE: The complete guide to live streaming for[33] **musicians**[34]

8. Offer free live streaming concerts with a tip jar

If you do not feel comfortable asking for payment up front for your live stream shows, hosting it for free and setting up a virtual tip jar is a wonderful way to go.

ON Facebook Live [35]and Instagram Live, [36]this can be as simple as sharing your PayPal link, Venmo username, or website link with your viewers. Or you could opt for a platform like Twitch [37]with built-in monetization features. Here's a full breakdown of how to[38] monetize each of the most popular live streaming[39] platforms.[40]

9. Monetize your Facebook and Instagram videos

A lot of musicians do not realize that they can earn money when their music is used in videos on Facebook and Instagram, just like on YouTube. You can even get paid when people use your songs in their Instagram Stories.

CHECK WITH YOUR DIGITAL distribution company to make sure they offer social video monetization[41].

---

33. https://bandzoogle.com/blog/the-complete-guide-to-live-streaming-for-musicians

34. https://bandzoogle.com/blog/the-complete-guide-to-live-streaming-for-musicians

35. https://diymusician.cdbaby.com/social-media/complete-facebook-live-toolkit-musicians/

36. https://diymusician.cdbaby.com/social-media/instagram-live-musicians/

37. https://diymusician.cdbaby.com/social-media/twitch-for-musicians/

38. https://bandzoogle.com/blog/the-complete-guide-to-live-streaming-for-musicians

39. https://bandzoogle.com/blog/the-complete-guide-to-live-streaming-for-musicians

40. https://bandzoogle.com/blog/the-complete-guide-to-live-streaming-for-musicians

10. Sell digital merch

There's so much more you can include in your band[42] merch store [43]than the standard t-shirts, posters, and stickers. Challenge yourself to think beyond physical goods and explore possibilities like digital sheet music[44] downloads[45], video lessons, or a nicely designed e-book of your lyrics.

YOU CAN BUILD YOUR very own merch store in minutes[46] with Bandzoogle[47]. It will be integrated right into your website, and as always, every sale you make is commission-free.

11. License your music

Getting your songs licensed for films, TV shows, and ads is easier said than done, [48]but even one placement could be a game changer for your music career. Some musicians earn most or all their income from licensing alone.

HITTING THE RIGHT MUSIC supervisor with the right song at the right time certainly involves some luck, but there are a few things you can do to increase your chances.[49]

Concluding thoughts

---

41. https://cdbaby.com/social-video-monetization.aspx

42.   https://bandzoogle.com/blog/the-ultimate-guide-to-selling-band-merch-online

43.   https://bandzoogle.com/blog/the-ultimate-guide-to-selling-band-merch-online

44.   https://bandzoogle.com/blog/how-to-sell-sheet-music-through-your-website

45.   https://bandzoogle.com/blog/how-to-sell-sheet-music-through-your-website

46. https://bandzoogle.com/features/sell-band-merch

47. https://bandzoogle.com/features/sell-band-merch

48.   https://aristake.com/?post=105

49. https://diymusician.cdbaby.com/musician-tips/wildly-successful-licensing-songs-tv-film-ads/

Do not feel like you must throw yourself into everything at once. Some of these ideas might be more doable for you than others, depending on the kind of musician you are, how far along you are in your career, and what your big-picture goals are.

Chapter 22

Reasons to Write a Press Release

If you have done any reading on the subject, you realize that sending out press releases is one of the most effective, cost-free strategies available for marketing your business. All too often, however, we just cannot think of why to send a release. We are under the mistaken impression that we simply have no newsworthy to share. Here is a list of sixty-five reasons to send out a press release that will help dispel that notion and help you get started today in utilizing this outstanding promotional strategy for your business:

o A contest you are sponsoring o A contest you have won

o A grant you are giving

o A grant you have received

o A scholarship you are contributing to o A scholarship you are sponsoring

o An award or commendation you have received o An award or commendation your company has received

o Appearance at national events o Articles written about you

o Articles you have written

o Awards you are handing out o Business Anniversary

o Business expansion

o Business Open House

o Change in business hours

o Classes you are teaching

o Classes your company is sponsoring

o Clients, or customers you have acquired o Company events or programs

o Company name change

o Company sponsored trip for your employees o Company tours you make available

o Contributions you are making to a local charity o Corporate accomplishments

o corporate sponsorships (sports teams, etc.) o Ezine or newsletter you publish

o Facilities Expansion o Free classes you offer

o Free demonstrations you are putting on

o Free information available at your website o Free samples you are offering

o Fundraiser you are sponsoring

o Guest you have invited to speak to your employees o Holiday promotions

o Holiday tie-ins

o Joint venture with another company o Key employees' retirement

o new employees you have hired

o New products or services you are offering

o New website or online service you are offering o Participate in local events

o Patents you have applied for or been awarded o Personal accomplishments

o Polls and surveys you have taken

o Publications you have to offer online or in print o Report on a fundraiser you finished

o Research you have conducted and the results

o Sales promotions

o Speaking engagements you have planned o Special events you are participating in

o Special events you are promoting o Special meetings you are hosting o the latest book that mentions you

o Trade shows you are participating in

o Trademarks you have applied for or been awarded o Training seminars you are attending

o TV show appearances

o Visits by local celebrities o Website anniversary

o Workshops you are presenting

o Your appointment to a board or committee o Your company's incorporation

o Your latest book o Your Retirement

Chapter 23

Testimonials and Reviews

BUT, RIGHT NOW WE ARE here to talk about a more straightforward approach to a page you may or may not have on your site, but I guarantee you have at least seen on other sites: the Press/Testimonials page. This is where you collect all the wonderful things other people have said about you in one handy place, so someone who does not know you can learn more about you while getting a good impression of you, and you can boast about yourself without boasting. It is a neat little trick.

But, like anything else, there are some effortless ways to screw it up. So here are some things to keep in mind when curating your press page:

Consider your sources.

If you get a positive review in the local paper, that is an easy decision. Post it. Helpful review from a blog that has a decent readership? I would say post it. An encouraging email from your uncle? I would skip that one. The idea here is that someone whose job it is to know about music thought your music was good. Or at least that is how I see it. I have come across instances where people post positive messages from random Facebook fans, and if I am being honest, that does not hold much weight with me.

But, in the end, that is your call. At its most basic level, this is nothing more than "This person liked my music. You are also a person. You will like it, too." And if you are all fired up about the positive reaction you are getting, then by all means: share those comments with the world. Just keep in mind that when those names are followed by "Denver Tribune" or whatever, they are going to resonate as more legit to those in the "industry.

Too few? Might look sad. Too many? Stop patting yourself on the back.

I have seen press pages that seem like they scroll on forever, and while that is a great problem to have, you do not want to overwhelm people with a huge wall of text on *any* page within your site. Take the ones that carry the most weight – or the most recent or relevant ones – and feature those.

Conversely, if you have only one quote, you may not want to dedicate a whole page to it. Find a unique way to feature it on your site – on your music page or in your header image – and then give it its own home when it has a few friends.

Testimonials from famous people, even if technically true, can come off as reaching.

Let us see if I can explain this one: I have seen testimonials artists have on their websites containing a generic-ish quote from a musician who seems *out* of their league. I am not going to pull up a real example, but it would be something like "'This guy can play!' – Carlos Santana." That may have happened. You met Carlos, knocked out a few licks for him, and he said something nice to you. But if it is not something you can attribute to an actual source, it might come off like you are padding your resume a bit.

Again: not to say you should not do that, but just consider how a Carlos Santana endorsement looks next to two pull quotes from a small-time blog. Fishy. And if someone went up to Carlos and asked him about you, would he immediately know who you are and repeat those words of praise? Yes? Then run with it. If not, you may want to just keep that awesome story (and it is awesome, make no mistake) to yourself.

If you are going to post your bad reviews, make sure you know what you are doing.

There's a way to take a bad review and spin it to your advantage, but there's also a way to take a bad review, attempt to spin it to your advantage, and only manage to direct a bunch of people to a bad review that they might not have seen had you not so conveniently pointed it out to them.

If some goon posts a ridiculous dressing-down of your entire operation and it is so far out of leftfield that you just *know* your fans will think it is funny, that is one thing. But if someone writes a coherent piece about why your show was terrible, citing numerous examples that you cannot refute, you might want to just leave it alone.

Chapter 24

Pay to Play in Today's Music Venues

1. Introduction

Pay to Play in music venues is a practice that involves artists paying a fee to perform live. This section will provide a comprehensive understanding of Pay to Play, including its definition, history, and evolution. It will also explore the impact of this practice on artists and the music industry. Furthermore, the section will analyze the pros and cons of Pay to Play, considering the advantages it offers for artists as well as the disadvantages they may face. Additionally, it will examine the benefits and drawbacks of Pay to Play presents for music venues. The strategies artists can implement to navigate this system will also be discussed, including building a passionate fan base, networking with other artists, and negotiating favorable deals. Finally, the section will touch upon the future of Pay to Play in music venues, considering emerging alternatives, potential changes in the industry and venue practices, and the challenge of balancing the need for exposure and fair compensation.

1.1 Definition of Pay to Play

Pay to Play refers to a practice in music venues where artists are required to pay a fee to perform. This payment is typically in exchange for a certain amount of stage time or the opportunity to open for a more established act. The concept has evolved over time, with its origins dating back to the late 20th century. Pay to Play can have both advantages and disadvantages for artists. On the one hand, it provides an opportunity for exposure and access to a larger audience. On the other hand, it can place a financial burden on artists, especially those who are just starting out. Music venues also experience benefits and drawbacks from this practice. Some argue that Pay to Play is an unfair business model that exploits artists, while others believe it is a necessary component of the music industry. To navigate Pay to Play, artists can employ strategies such as building a passionate fan base, networking with other artists, and negotiating favorable deals. The future of Pay to Play in music venues remains uncertain, as emerging alternatives and potential changes in the industry may shift the dynamics of this practice. Balancing the need for exposure and fair compensation will continue to be an ongoing challenge for artists and music venues alike.

1.2 History and Evolution of Pay to Play in Music Venues

During its history, pay to play in music venues has undergone significant changes. In the past, it was common for artists to pay a fee to secure a performance slot at a venue. This practice often left artists with little or no profit from their performances. Over time, however, the music industry has seen a shift towards more artist-friendly practices. Many venues now prioritize fair compensation for artists and offer opportunities for them to earn revenue through ticket sales or merchandise. Despite these positive changes, pay to play still presents challenges for artists, as they must navigate the balance between exposure and fair compensation. In the evolving music industry, alternative approaches to pay to play are emerging, and potential future changes in venue practices may further address the need for fair compensation while still providing opportunities for artists to gain exposure.

1.3 Impact of Pay to Play on Artists and the Music Industry

The impact of pay to play on artists and the music industry is significant. On the one hand, it provides artists with an opportunity to showcase their talent and gain exposure to a wider audience. It allows them to build connections and potentially attract industry professionals. However, pay to play can also be detrimental to artists as it places a financial burden on them, often requiring them to pay upfront fees without any guarantee of compensation. This can result in financial losses and discouragement for emerging artists. Furthermore, the prevalence of pay to play in music venues has contributed to a devaluation of live performances, leading to a decrease in overall artist compensation. It is crucial for artists and the music industry to find a balance between exposure and fair compensation to ensure the sustainability and growth of the industry.

2. The Pros and Cons of Pay to Play

Pay to Play in today's music venues has both advantages and disadvantages for artists. On the positive side, participating in Pay to Play allows for increased exposure and the opportunity to perform in established venues. It can also serve as a platform for building a fan base and connecting with other artists. However, there are also downsides to Pay to Play. Artists may find themselves incurring financial costs without receiving fair compensation for their performances. Additionally, the practice can perpetuate a system where artists are expected to pay for opportunities, rather than being paid for their talent. Both artists and music venues must carefully weigh the benefits and drawbacks before engaging in Pay to Play arrangements.

2.1 Advantages of Pay to Play for Artists There are several advantages for artists when it comes to participating in the pay to play model in music venues. Firstly, it provides an opportunity for exposure and reaching a wider audience. By performing in established venues, artists can showcase their talent to a diverse crowd who may not have discovered them otherwise. Additionally, pay to play allows artists to build connections and network within the industry. Performing alongside other talented musicians can lead to collaborations and future opportunities. Furthermore, pay to play can serve as a steppingstone for artists to gain experience and improve their stage presence. It offers a platform to hone their performance skills and refine their craft. Lastly, some venues offer a percentage of the ticket sales or potential revenue sharing, providing a financial incentive for artists to participate in the pay to play model. Overall, while there are criticisms of pay to play, it does offer distinct advantages for artists looking to establish themselves in the music industry.

2.2 Disadvantages of Pay to Play for Artists Pay to Play may seem like a way for artists to gain exposure and opportunities, but it comes with several disadvantages. Firstly, artists are often required to pay upfront fees to perform, putting financial strain on those who may not have the means. Additionally, these fees are often nonrefundable, meaning artists have nothing to show for their investment if the performance does not go well. Furthermore, Pay to Play can create a negative perception of the artist's worth, as they are paying for the chance to perform. This can undermine their credibility and potential for future paid gigs. Lastly, Pay to Play may contribute to a culture where talent and merit take a backseat to financial resources, limiting opportunities for up-and-coming artists.

2.3 Benefits and Drawbacks for Music Venues Some music venues see benefits in implementing pay-to-play policies. By charging artists to perform, venues can generate revenue and cover expenses. Additionally, pay to play can ensure that artists are serious and committed, resulting in higher quality performances. However, there are drawbacks to this practice as well. It can create financial barriers for up-and-coming artists who may not have the funds to pay for gigs. Furthermore, pay to play can devalue the work of musicians by suggesting that exposure is more important than fair compensation. Music venues must carefully consider both the benefits and drawbacks of implementing pay to play policies to create a balanced and fair environment for artists.

3. Strategies for Artists to Navigate Pay to Play 1. Building a Strong Fan Base and Online Presence: By actively engaging with fans on social media and promoting their music online, artists can increase their visibility and attract a dedicated following. This can make them more appealing to music venues and give them leverage when negotiating pay to play deals.

2. NETWORKING AND COLLABORATING with Other Artists: By connecting with like-minded musicians and collaborating on projects, artists can expand their network and gain access to new opportunities. This can lead to more bookings at music venues and potential partnerships that can help offset the costs of pay to play.

3. Negotiating Favorable Pay to Play Deals: Artists should approach pay to play arrangements with a business mindset and negotiate terms that are fair and beneficial for both parties. This includes discussing the number of tickets required to be sold, the ticket price, and any additional rewards such as merchandise sales or a percentage of the bar revenue.

By implementing these strategies, artists can navigate the challenges of pay to play and increase their chances of success in today's music venues.

3.1 BUILDING A STRONG Fan Base and Online Presence Building a passionate fan base and online presence is crucial for artists navigating the pay to play system in today's music venues. By cultivating a dedicated following and engaging with fans online, artists can create a demand for their music and increase their chances of getting booked for shows. Social media platforms and streaming services provide opportunities for artists to connect with fans, share their music, and promote upcoming performances. Additionally, utilizing email marketing and attending live events are effective ways for artists to expand their fan base and generate buzz. In an industry where exposure is key, establishing a strong online presence and cultivating a loyal fan base can help artists navigate the challenges of the pay to play model and increase their chances of success.

3.2 Networking and Collaborating with Other Artists Networking and collaborating with other artists is

a crucial strategy for musicians to navigate the pay to play system in today's music venues. By connecting with other artists, musicians can not only expand their fan base but also gain access to valuable resources and opportunities. Collaborations allow artists to pool their skills and talents, creating a unique and powerful musical experience that can attract a larger audience. Networking with other artists also provides a support system within the industry, where artists can share knowledge, contacts, and advice. Moreover, collaborating with established artists can open doors to more prestigious gigs and better paying opportunities. By working together, artists can navigate the challenges of pay to play and enhance their overall success in the music industry.

3.3 Negotiating Favorable Pay to Play Deals When negotiating pay-to-play deals in today's music venues, artists should employ several key strategies to ensure favorable outcomes. Firstly, artists should carefully research and evaluate potential venues to ensure they align with their target audience and musical style. This will create a stronger bargaining position and increase the chances of attracting a supportive audience. Additionally, building strong relationships with venue owners and promoters can lead to better negotiating opportunities. Artists should also consider collaborating with other musicians to share costs and increase their collective bargaining power. Furthermore, artists should clearly communicate their expectations and goals, specifying the desired compensation and any additional benefits they seek. Finally, artists should be prepared to negotiate and potentially walk away from deals that do not align with their financial or artistic objectives. By implementing these strategies, artists can navigate pay-to-play arrangements more effectively and secure favorable outcomes.

4. The Future of Pay to Play in Music Venues As the music industry continues to evolve, the future of pay to play in music venues is uncertain. There are emerging alternatives to the pay to play model, such as crowdfunding campaigns and streaming platforms, which provide artists with new opportunities for exposure and compensation. Additionally, potential changes in the music industry and venue practices, such as increased support for independent artists and fairer compensation models, could impact the prevalence of pay to play. However, finding the balance between the need for exposure and fair compensation remains a challenge. Artists must continue to adapt and explore different strategies, such as building a passionate fan base, networking with other artists, and negotiating favorable pay to play deals, in order to navigate the changing landscape of music venues.

4.1 Emerging Alternatives to Pay to Play Emerging alternatives to pay-to-play in today's music venues are beginning to gain traction. One such alternative is the concept of "pay-to-stream" shows, where artists can showcase their performances through live streaming platforms and earn revenue through virtual ticket sales. This allows artists to reach a wider audience without the need for physical venues or the financial burden of pay-to-play arrangements. Additionally, some music venues are experimenting with new models that prioritize fair compensation for artists, such as revenue sharing agreements based on ticket sales or providing guaranteed minimum payments. These alternatives have the potential to disrupt the pay-to-play model and create more equitable opportunities for artists in the music industry. However, the long-term sustainability and widespread adoption of these emerging alternatives are still uncertain, as they require support and collaboration from both artists and music venues.

4.2 POTENTIAL CHANGES in the Music Industry and Venue Practices

As the music industry continues to evolve, there are several potential changes in the industry and venue practices that could impact the pay to play model. One potential change is the shift towards more artist-friendly practices, with venues recognizing the need to support artists financially rather than relying solely on pay to play deals. This could involve offering fair compensation for performances or providing other forms of support such as marketing and promotion. Additionally, advancements in technology and the rise of streaming platforms may provide alternative avenues for artists to gain exposure and generate income, reducing the reliance on traditional music venues. Finally, there may be a shift towards more curated and specialized venues that focus on specific genres or niche audiences, offering artists a more targeted and engaged fan base. Overall, these potential changes could lead to a more equitable and supportive environment for artists in the music industry.

4.3 Balancing the Need for Exposure and Fair Compensation

In today's music venues, finding a balance between exposure and fair compensation is crucial for both artists and venues. Pay to Play arrangements have both advantages and disadvantages for artists, allowing them to gain exposure but also potentially exploiting their talent. Music venues also benefit from Pay to Play, as it guarantees revenue and attracts a larger audience. Artists can navigate Pay to Play by building a passionate fan base and online presence, networking with other artists, and negotiating favorable deals.

However, the future of Pay to Play is uncertain, as emerging alternatives and potential changes in the music industry and venue practices may shift the balance towards fair compensation for artists. Ultimately, finding the right balance between exposure and fair compensation is necessary for a thriving music industry.

Chapter 25

Strategies for Securing Gigs in the Music Business

1. BUILDING A STRONG Network

Building a strong network is essential for securing gigs in the music business. Attending industry events and conferences allows you to connect with key industry players and potential collaborators. Joining musician associations and organizations provides access to valuable resources and networking opportunities. Collaborating with other musicians and bands can expand your network and create new opportunities for gigs. Utilizing social media platforms for networking helps you reach a wider audience and connect with industry professionals. By focusing on building a strong network, you increase your chances of securing gigs and advancing your music career.

1.1. Attending industry events and conferences Attending industry events and conferences is a key strategy for securing gigs in the music business. By attending these events, musicians can connect with industry professionals, network with other musicians, and showcase their talent. These events often attract talent scouts, booking agents, and other industry insiders who can potentially offer gigs or recommend musicians for future opportunities. By actively participating in industry events and conferences, musicians can increase their visibility and establish valuable connections that can lead to gig opportunities.

1.2. JOIN MUSICIAN associations and organizations One effective strategy for securing gigs in the music business is to join musician associations

and organizations. These associations can provide valuable networking opportunities and resources for musicians looking to showcase their talent and connect with industry professionals. By becoming a member, musicians gain access to events, workshops, and conferences where they can meet other like-minded musicians and potentially form collaborations. Additionally, these associations often have online forums or directories where musicians can promote their work and connect with potential gig opportunities. Overall, joining musician associations and organizations is a proactive way for musicians to expand their network, gain exposure, and increase their chances of securing gigs in the music industry.

1.3. Collaborate with other musicians and bands Collaborating with other musicians and bands is an effective strategy for securing gigs in the music business. By working together, musicians can pool their resources and networks to reach a larger audience and increase their chances of getting booked. Collaborations can take various forms, such as performing together at shows, co-writing songs, or even creating joint promotional campaigns. This not only exposes each artist to new fans but also enhances their credibility and marketability. When collaborating, it is important for musicians to find partners whose musical style aligns with theirs and who have a strong work ethic. By building symbiotic relationships with other musicians and bands, artists can expand their reach and increase their opportunities for booking gigs.

1.4. Utilize social media platforms for networking When it comes to securing gigs in the music business, utilizing social media platforms for networking is essential. Social media allows musicians to connect with fans, industry professionals, and other musicians, expanding

their network and increasing their visibility. By consistently posting updates, sharing music and videos, and engaging with followers, musicians can build a loyal fan base and attract the attention of industry professionals. Social media also offers opportunities for collaboration with other musicians and bands, leading to potential gig opportunities. Additionally, platforms like Facebook Events and Instagram Live can be used to promote upcoming shows and connect with local venues and festivals, increasing the chances of securing bookings. By leveraging the power of social media, musicians can effectively network and build relationships in the music industry, leading to more gig opportunities.

2. Promoting Yourself Effectively

To promote yourself effectively in the music business, there are several key strategies to implement. Firstly, creating a professional press kit is essential. This includes a well-crafted biography, high-quality promotional photos, and samples of your music. Additionally, developing an engaging online presence is crucial. Utilize social media platforms to share your music, connect with fans, and engage with industry professionals. Submitting your music to local venues and festivals can also help raise your profile and secure gigs. Lastly, word-of-mouth recommendations hold great power in the industry. Focus on providing memorable live performances and encouraging fans to spread the word about your music. By implementing these strategies, you will increase your chances of securing gigs and building a successful career in the music business.

2.1. CREATE A PROFESSIONAL press kit.

A professional press kit is an essential tool for musicians looking to secure gigs in the music business. It provides potential venues and promoters with a comprehensive overview of your talent, experience, and brand. When creating a press kit, include a professional biography,

high-quality promotional photos, samples of your music, and any press coverage or reviews you have received. Make sure to highlight your unique selling points and showcase your best work. Having a well-curated and visually appealing press kit will help grab the attention of industry professionals and increase your chances of securing gigs.

2.2. Develop an engaging online presence Developing an engaging online presence is crucial for musicians looking to secure gigs in the music business. By creating and maintaining a strong online presence, artists can showcase their music, connect with fans and industry professionals, and attract the attention of potential booking agents and venues. This can be achieved through various strategies such as creating an appealing website or social media profiles, regularly sharing high-quality content, including music videos and live performances, and engaging with followers through comments and messages. Additionally, musicians can utilize online platforms and streaming services to reach a wider audience and gain exposure. By consistently developing and promoting their online presence, musicians increase their chances of securing gigs and building a successful career in the music industry.

2.3. Submit your music to local venues and festivals To increase your chances of securing gigs in the

music business, it is vital to submit your music to local venues and festivals. This allows you to showcase your talent to a wider audience and gain exposure in your community. When submitting your music, ensure that you follow the submission guidelines provided by the venues and festivals. This may include sending demo recordings, press kits, and other promotional materials. It is also important to tailor your submissions to match the style and preferences of each venue or festival. By targeting the right audience, you can increase your chances of being selected to perform and build valuable connections within the industry. Remember to be patient and persistent in your submissions, as it may take time to receive responses. Overall, submitting your music to local venues and festivals is a proactive way to get your foot in the door and start building your reputation as a musician.

2.4. Leverage the power of word-of-mouth recommendations to secure gigs in the music business, leveraging the power of word-of-mouth recommendations is crucial. When satisfied customers and industry professionals spread positive reviews about your performances, it can significantly enhance your chances of getting booked for future gigs. One way to encourage word-of-mouth recommendations is by consistently delivering outstanding live performances that leave an impression on the audience. Additionally, building strong relationships with fellow musicians, venue owners, and managers can lead to valuable referrals. Actively engaging with your fans on social media platforms and encouraging them to share their experiences can also help generate positive word-of-mouth. This strategy can expand your network and increase your visibility within the music industry, opening doors to more opportunities for gigs.

3. Establishing Relationships with Venues

To secure gigs in the music business, it is crucial to establish relationships with venues. Research and target suitable venues for your genre and build relationships with their owners and managers. Offer to perform for free or at a discounted rate initially to showcase your talent and prove your worth. By providing high-quality live performances, you can ensure repeat bookings and establish yourself as a reliable and talented musician. Additionally, understanding the booking process and requirements, negotiating fair contracts and agreements, maintaining open communication with venue representatives, and keeping track of your bookings are essential for navigating the booking process and securing future opportunities.

3.1. Research and target suitable venues for your genre When looking to secure gigs in the music

business, it is important to research and target suitable venues for your genre. This involves analyzing the types of venues that typically host your style of music and identifying the ones that align with your target audience. By understanding the venues that are known for catering to your genre, you can increase your chances of getting booked and reaching the right audience. Researching venues also allows you to gather information on their booking process and requirements, enabling you to approach them in a professional and informed manner. Additionally, targeting suitable venues helps you establish a reputation within a specific music scene and build connections with venue owners and managers, which can lead to future booking opportunities. Remember, securing gigs is not just about showcasing your talent, but also about understanding the market and identifying the right platforms to showcase your music effectively.

3.2. Build relationships with venue owners and managers
Building relationships with venue owners and managers is crucial for securing gigs in the music business. By establishing a personal connection and rapport, you increase the likelihood of being considered for future performances. When approaching venues, it is important to research and target those that align with your genre and target audience. Additionally, offering to perform for free or at a discounted rate initially can demonstrate your talent and dedication while building trust with venue owners. Once you have secured a gig, providing high-quality live performances is essential for ensuring repeat bookings. Communication is key throughout the booking process, so maintaining open and professional communication with venue representatives is crucial. Finally, keeping track of your bookings and following up for future opportunities will help you continue to build your career in the music industry.

3.3. Offer to perform for free or at a discounted rate initially
One effective strategy for securing gigs in the music business is to offer to perform for free or at a discounted rate initially. By doing so, musicians can demonstrate their talent and build a reputation

within the industry. This can lead to future paid opportunities and increased exposure. Additionally, offering to perform for free or at a discounted rate can help musicians establish relationships with venue owners and managers, who may be more willing to book them in the future. It is important for musicians to provide high-quality live performances during these initial gigs to ensure repeat bookings and positive word-of-mouth recommendations. By utilizing this strategy, musicians can effectively navigate the booking process and establish themselves within the music industry.

3.4. Provide high-quality live performances to ensure repeat bookings.

To secure repeat bookings in the music business, it is essential to deliver high-quality live performances. This requires musicians to consistently showcase their talent, energy, and stage presence during each gig. By putting on memorable shows, artists can leave an impression on both the audience and venue owners. This positive experience increases the likelihood of being rebooked for future gigs. To ensure high-quality performances, musicians should focus on their musical proficiency, stage craft, and professionalism. By continuously honing their skills and maintaining a strong work ethic, artists can build a reputation for delivering exceptional live shows, leading to more opportunities in the industry.

4. Navigating the Booking Process

To successfully navigate the booking process in the music business, it is crucial to have a clear understanding of the process and its requirements. This involves researching suitable venues for your genre, building relationships with venue owners and managers, and offering to perform for free or at a discounted rate initially. It is also important to negotiate fair contracts and agreements, maintain open communication with venue representatives, and provide high-quality live performances to ensure repeat bookings. Additionally, keeping track of your bookings and following up for future opportunities is essential for securing gigs in the music industry.

4.1. Understand the booking process and requirements to secure gigs in the music business, it is

important to understand the booking process and requirements. This involves familiarizing oneself with how venues book musicians and what they look for in potential performers. Additionally, it is crucial to negotiate fair contracts and agreements to protect one's interests. Maintaining open communication with venue representatives is essential for a successful booking experience, as it allows for any necessary adjustments or clarifications. To stay organized, it is recommended to keep track of all bookings and follow-up for future opportunities. By thoroughly understanding and navigating the booking process, musicians can increase their chances of securing gigs and building their careers in the music industry.

4.2. Negotiate fair contracts and agreements When securing gigs in the music business, it is crucial to negotiate fair contracts and agreements. This involves discussing payment terms, performance expectations, and any specific requirements. It is important to carefully review the contract and seek legal advice if needed. It is also essential to maintain open communication with venue representatives throughout the negotiation process. By effectively negotiating contracts and agreements, musicians can

ensure a fair and mutually beneficial arrangement with venues, helping to establish a professional reputation and secure future opportunities.

4.3. Maintain open communication with venue representatives Maintain open communication with venue representatives by actively engaging in regular communication and updates. Respond promptly to emails, phone calls, or any other form of communication from venue representatives. Keep them informed about any changes or updates regarding your availability or performance details. This open line of communication will help build trust and strengthen your professional relationship with the venue. Additionally, try to attend meetings or face-to-face interactions with venue representatives whenever possible. This can provide an opportunity to discuss any concerns or suggestions and ensure that both parties are on the same page. Remember, clear and open communication is key to securing gigs and establishing a successful partnership with venues.

4.4. Keep track of your bookings and follow-up for future opportunities.

To ensure future opportunities in the music business, it is crucial to keep track of your bookings and consistently follow up. Maintaining organized records of your gigs allows you to stay on top of your schedule and availability. By doing so, you can effectively plan and prepare for future performances. Additionally, following up with venue representatives after a gig shows professionalism and a desire to continue working together. This can lead to future bookings and collaborations. By keeping track of your bookings and regularly following up, you demonstrate your commitment to your craft.

Chapter 26

Best Way to Promote Your Live Show

Action Plan

1. Make a list of everyone in your network.

2. Try to sell tickets to your show to every person on the list

3. Encourage each of those people to put together a list of people and to encourage those people to come to the show.

4. Of the founding members of your fan base create a street team to help promote you.

5. Keep a list and update that list of all contacts

They will be the most passionate about spreading your name and inviting their friends to show, and they will be happy to see your success grow. This is how you are quickly going to start drawing 50-100+ fans to every show you put on.

Make sure EACH member of your group is proactive, involved, and doing their share of the promotion workload. Have each member carry around physical tickets and fliers everywhere they go. Assign each member specific promo tasks or goals.

Each member should invite every person they see face-to-face during their normal activities to the show, focusing especially on people they already know. Do not just hand out fliers and walk off. Spend a few minutes with them, make them feel special, and invite them to your show. When you are face-to-face with somebody interested in attending, be sure to SELL THEM A TICKET at once. You can easily turn a friend from "I think I'll show up, it sounds fun!" to buy 1 ticket for themselves and 1-2 tickets for their friends right there on the spot. This will not happen unless you ask!

Normally, advance tickets are cheaper than door prices – so you save your fans money when you see them in person! Any time that you spend doing this is an investment that will yield a high return. You are spreading the word, making social connections, and building a social world.

Use your contacts by texting, calling, or messaging about your show. It is proven that texting is the most successful way. Your network is the foundation of your large and ever-growing fan base.

You Know a Lot of People.

Research has shown that the average American knows about 300 people. You collectively have A LOT of social capital in your networks. Sit down with your group and have each member MAKE A LIST of every person they know in your area. Go through your phone contacts, email contacts, and list of Facebook friends. I have always, wholeheartedly, believed that any local artist can draw 15-20 fans at the VERY least. Truthfully, I believe most local artists can and should be able to draw 50+ people per show. All you must do is focus on smart promoting with tactics that yield results rather than blindly wasting time passing out fliers to strangers. This action plan COSTS YOU NOTHING. Just be smart, work hard, and focus on the people who are most likely to help you succeed.

Some reasons to buy are:

1. Advance tickets save you money (If promo code discounts are active, they will save you even more).

2. The sooner you buy, things will happen for my band (more pay, better time slot, longer set, the club/promoter will be impressed, I will get more shows or be rebooked if we have impressive ticket sales.

3. This show is important / means a lot to me.

4. This show is special (B-day show, CD release, amazing venue or lineup, new songs, etc.)

5. You can offer fans INCENTIVES (free CD, one free song, signed poster, song dedication, pre-show party or after-show party invite, etc.) if they purchase tickets early or buy tickets in group bundles.

The more personal you are when you reach out, the more effective your promo time will be. Email blasts and Facebook Event blasts at this point yield exceptionally low results because people are numb to notifications and mass marketing. A person "Attending" on a Facebook Event is less likely to show up than a person who buys a ticket in advance. Social media and Facebook Events give an illusion that a bunch of people are coming to your show.

A wonderful way to keep track is to cross names off your list as friends/fans say they cannot attend and highlight or circle friends who have bought tickets. This way you know WHO TO FOLLOW UP WITH! Ask friends who bought tickets if they can bring along more friends and carpool.

Always Give A "Call to Action."

Always give a "call to action." Here is what I mean by this. During your personal 1-on-1 invitation, ask the person to do something or respond with an answer. This way the person feels engaged and feels like they need to reply to you. Here are some "call to action" examples:

If you buy a ticket by X date, I can get you a FREE CD. Do you already have a copy?

I am trying to keep track of who can go so I know who I can count on. Are you coming for sure?

If you bring 3 friends to my show, I can comp your ticket or give you a free merch item.

While you are deciding if you can go, can you SHARE my show poster on your FB page?

Which song would you most like to hear?"

Anything that is a call to action and asks for a response or for a decision to be made is going to yield much higher results. This also puts you into a 1-on-1, back-and-forth conversation with your friends and fans. Even if a friend cannot attend, you can still ask them to post about the show, invite their friends, or put you in contact with anybody they know who would like your band!

Get Each Ticket Buyer to Bring Out Their Friends!

Your fans and friends care about you. They WANT to help you. When you reach out to them and ask them to bring friends tell them about the incentives if they do so.

The fans who have already bought tickets ARE 100% going to your show, so the next step is to ask them to BRING THEIR FRIENDS. Nobody likes going to a show alone, right? If a couple is coming, don't they have 2 open seats in their car?

Start treating your existing fans like VIPs. Create some EXISTING FAN DEALS with incentives if they bring people to your show who have never seen you perform live. Investing $0.50 for a fan to bring you a new fan OR $5 – $10 in free stuff for a fan to bring you FIVE new fans is completely worth it! Be creative in what you offer and how you word it.

The (Your Act Name Here) Bring Friends Deal:

Bring (1) friend who is never seen us perform = FREE Sticker + 1 or 2-Song CD Sampler

Bring (3) friends who have never seen us perform = FREE Sticker + Full Length CD

Bring (5) friends who have never seen us perform.

= The Above + FREE T-SHIRT + I will buy your 1st drink!

Bring (10) friends who have never seen us perform.

= All Above + Song Dedication + We will pay for your ticket

Once you start doing this, some friends/fans will end up bringing you 5, 10, 15+ new fans over just a few shows. They will keep bringing new friends to your shows. Why? Because they are going to start seeing how big of an impact they are having on your success and how happy that makes you. Your friends and fans WANT TO HELP YOU – they just need a little incentive push to get started.

That Snowball Effect.

If you build the foundation of your fan base by starting with your network and people you already know you can then leverage your social world in a big way. You can work outward from the people you DO know into the networks of their friends and people you DON'T KNOW yet. This type of grassroots strategy creates what we like to call the Snowball Effect it grows and picks up speed.

You Are Not Done Yet.

Many artists think their show promotion ends once the show starts. This is NOT the case. Your promo action plan for this show does not end until the show itself ends.

You have worked so hard to sell 25, 35, 50+ Tickets. You now have, for certain, a large crowd of people showing up. They all know you and are excited to cheer you on. Think about how impressive that looks to every other fan and band in the venue on the night of the show. Everyone else has a sparse, barely clapping crowd. But you, due to your excellent promotional work, are going to have a densely packed crowd up against the stage shouting and cheering you on.

That is going to turn heads and immediately make other bands' fans stop and take you seriously.

This is where you are going to make new fans out of the other bands' fans. First impression? You are a band with a buzz because you have an impressive crowd. The room is not awkward or sparse. It is now easier to get other bands' fans to move forward, join the crowd, and engage in your live performance.

MANY LOCAL ARTISTS show up and expect their music and live performance to win over everyone in the room. It might... But usually, it takes more than that, some type of personal connection or crowd engagement.

Before You Perform

1. Make a point to introduce yourself personally and MEET as many of the other bands' fans as you can before you go onstage.

2. Tell them which act you are in and what time you perform. If they are not super interested move on, if there is a connection chat a couple of minutes.

3. Tell them that if they stay for your set, you will give them free merch at your merch table if they come to talk to you.

4. Keep an email list and ask everybody if they would like to be notified of upcoming events and updates.

Chapter 27

Corporate Sponsors

ATTRACTING CORPORATE Sponsors

Genuine interest in working with a sponsor because they know the alliance will provide something of value for both organizations.

Conviction that they are offering a good marketing investment to the sponsor.

Nonprofits need to price their proposals on their promotional value to the corporate sponsor. Sponsors want to exploit the commercial opportunities associated with an event, cause, or organization.

Are You Ready for Corporate Sponsors? A Reality Check

To see if your organization is ready for a corporate sponsor follow this checklist:

- Do you have an established marketing effort in place so that you keep in touch with your constituents through e-mail, a website, events, newsletters, [1]conferences, television, radio, or print advertising?

- What do you know about your organization's demographics? Is there up-to-date information about

---

1. http://nonprofit.about.com/od/fundraising/fr/newslettersrev.htm

who participates and why? Where do they live? How far do they drive? Whether they are repeat users? Whether they are young families, empty nesters, or teens?

- Have you worked with corporate sponsors before? Do you have testimonials from corporate executives about the value of your organization? Do you feature those in press kits or other marketing materials?

- Are you a member of civic organizations made up of businesspeople, so that you can gain insight and entrée into the business community?

- Is there an entrepreneurial spirit in your organization? Are innovative ideas welcomed, and do they receive thoughtful consideration? Have other commercial or revenue-generating initiatives been realized over the past five years?

CORPORATE SPONSORSHIP—ALSO known as event marketing or cause marketing (in the case of sponsorship of nonprofit or charitable events)—is a new form of advertising in which companies pay to be associated with certain events. Corporate sponsorship has been growing rapidly in recent years; in fact, it grew at a faster rate than the growth in overall corporate advertising in the late 1990s. In addition to the advertising and promotion aspects of corporate sponsorship, it also provides benefits in the realm of community relations. A comprehensive, ongoing community relations program—including event sponsorship—can help any organization achieve visibility as a good community citizen. Organizations are recognized as good community citizens when they support programs that improve the quality of life in their community.

Event sponsorship is an attractive option because it provides a business with access to various audiences, including employees, business decision-makers, and government regulators as well as consumers. It can be an especially good marketing tool for companies that participate in international trade because sponsorship transcends language and cultural barriers. Many marketers feel that corporate sponsorship is superior to other methods because it allows for an immediate customer response to new product offerings. Events provide business managers with an opportunity to come face-to-face with their customers. They also provide customers with an opportunity to try a company's products out firsthand.

THE FEES INVOLVED IN event marketing can range from a few hundred dollars to hundreds of thousands of dollars, depending on the scale of the event and the level of the sponsor's involvement. In addition to the cost of staging the event itself, there are also associated advertising, publicity, and administrative costs to consider.

Many small businesses choose to begin as co-sponsors of an existing event, which allows them to take advantage of the other sponsors' experience. It may also be possible for a small business to underwrite a new event and share advertising costs with a co-sponsor. Some businesses find it difficult to justify the expense of corporate sponsorship because it can be difficult to gauge the results in monetary terms. But it is often possible to conduct before and after interviews with attendees of the event, or to give away coupons and then track redemption rates. Some businesses also attempt to gauge the success of an event by providing a toll-free telephone number for attendees to call for more information about their products or services.

How To Find and Pitch Yourself to A Sponsor

Gaining a sponsor is like getting a job. It is delicate and nuanced. What is different about gaining a sponsor is how you pitch yourself to them. Here are 5 guidelines to getting a sponsor, and 4 points to remember while pitching yourself to them.

1. Know your sponsor.

Think of every potential sponsor as a potential business partner. You are not friends, so you cannot show up at their building unannounced and expect they will welcome you with open arms. You must court their interest. The best way to do this is to learn as much as you can about their service or product. The next step is to build your pitch to them.

2. Who are you? What do you want? What can you do for them?

If you take nothing away from this article but these three questions, great. When calling, emailing, or approaching any sponsor they are going to want to know these three things. You should be able to effectively communicate that information to them concisely.

3. Contact sponsors you like/think you can help in your immediate area.

If you do not like a product, do not ask them to be your sponsor. Look for a company whose product or services you enjoy or like, because you will be talking about it, and promoting it. If you are not happy with the product, it will show when you try to sell it, and it will make you, and the company who is sponsoring you, look bad. Go with something you care about.

4. Outline your pitch with specifics

You should be able to tell your sponsor how much funding you will need and in exchange you will display their logo on your tour, on these specific dates. You will also work "mentions" of their product into the show. In exchange, you will offer to work at corporate events. Get specific and present it to them in your pitch. Make sure what you offer is not available to another artist like you.

5. Make sure you can do a lot for them

You are competing with other musicians for sponsors. If someone else who is as unique as you can offer more value to a sponsor, they are going with someone else, no matter how much heart you bring to the table. Make sure you provide a variety of value to your sponsor. Not just logos, mentions, or tickets for corporate executives. You can also create a music video for them to help sell their product. Get creative.

6. But how do I tell this to them? How do I write them a good pitch?

I am glad you would like to know. You take the principles I have outlined above, and you start with them in this order, writing in a basic cover letter format. You also lead with this when speaking directly with a potential sponsor in person.

Introduce who you are. What you want. What are your skills, and what you can DO FOR THEM?

This is crucial. A sponsor wants to know who you are, what kind of influence or specific skills you have that are of unique value, what you want from them, and what value you can add in return. Write this in the opening paragraph of your email, or when you speak to your sponsor face to face.

"Hi. I am Jim, from Category IV. We are a popular indie rock group based here in Zanesville. We would like to have you as a sponsor. In return, we will promote your product at every one of our shows during 2024. Take the time to get in there and show your sponsor that you are an established musician/group that has a lot to offer and would like to have them as a sponsor.

Tell them clearly what your audience is, and how this will help them. They do not want to sponsor someone whose audience is unemployed college students when they are selling timeshares at a beachside resort. Make sure your audience is their audience and tell them how this will work into their business target.

What are the market rewards for sponsoring you?

As I mentioned above, tell your potential sponsor what specific marketing incentives they have for using you. What do you have that someone else does not have? Are you a favorite at the local five-star hotel? That would be a fantastic location for a specific financial demographic. Tell them what you can offer in terms of marketing that no one else can.

Ultimately, how are you going to benefit the sponsor?

What is the result of investing money in you? What is the goal? Sales growth for the sponsor? Increased awareness of the product in a newer market? Or is it educating their established audience on a new product? What is the result going to be from all the effort you put in?

Put this all in a cover letter, email, or in writing for yourself to remember when you approach your sponsor.

Knowing and sticking to the principles outlined above and putting them in a professional written/verbal pitch will help you in obtaining a sponsor, the rest will have to be done by you. Good luck!

SET SPONSORSHIP LEVELS.

Make sure the benefits at each level are distinct and enticing enough to encourage previous sponsors to move up a level.

It is a clever idea to have a wide range of levels so that smaller businesses as well as larger companies can find a level that suits their needs and budget. If your event is quite small, your entry-level sponsors might simply receive a small ad in an accompanying program or flyer for $50. For larger events, sponsor levels might begin at $200, $500, or even $1,000. Depending on audience size and publicity opportunities, the cost of a "title" sponsorship could range from $750 to $10,000. Title sponsors receive maximum publicity, and their logos should appear in ALL publicity material.

You should base your sponsor levels on the benefits to the company. Put a price on each benefit you will offer and add the prices in each level. This will give you an idea of the cost of sponsorship at each level.

Know in advance that you may have to be flexible and customize levels for some sponsors to meet their marketing needs. Some sponsors might be interested in half cash, half in-kind (product donation) sponsorship. Food and beverage companies often would like to see their logo on T-shirts, hear their company name announced, etc. They may want to have a table or booth available to distribute their products.

Depending on your event, these are a few benefits you might want to consider offering.

• sponsor banner displayed at the event. • sponsor name announced at the event.

• dinner table supported by the sponsor (i.e., each person at the table receives a promotional item and literature from the sponsor and the sponsor's logo is displayed at the table).

• small sponsor banner or logo displayed on the podium.

• sponsor name or logo in the organization's newsletter.

• sponsor name or logo in advertisements in newspapers and magazines.

• sponsor ad in program or flyer (ad size can range from business-card size to full page).

• sponsor logo on the organization's website (can include a hotlink to their site).

- sponsor logo on T-shirt; and
- category exclusivity (a guarantee to sponsors that once they sign on, none of their competitors will be allowed to sponsor).

MAKE LOTS OF PHONE calls.

The most time-consuming—but money-saving—step: Get on the phone and pitch your event as a great marketing opportunity.

Call local businesses to find out if they are interested in reaching your market. When you begin your conversation, focus on how the company will benefit: "This is Such and Such from My Organization. I thought you might be interested in marketing your company's products/services at an upcoming event we are hosting...do you have a few seconds?" Produce a pitch that in 20 seconds OR LESS explains the event, audience, and some benefits to the company. If they are interested, you can always go into more detail or send more information.

Your calls will vary with the type and size of the company you contact. You will speak directly to owners of small local businesses. Medium-size companies may have marketing departments or human resource departments that take care of sponsorships. Large companies receive countless requests for sponsorship, and they may have a sponsorship recording that gives you their guidelines for requests. These companies usually put together their budgets once a year, often in October, so you may have to send your proposal months ahead of time. Be sure to pay attention to corporate areas of focus: Some companies make commitments to only sponsor certain groups such as children or environmental organizations.

For potential sponsor ideas, talk to your board, staff, and volunteers. Investigate their ideas and connections. Try contacting advertising and public relations agencies to see if they think any of their clients might be interested in your event. See if any events like yours or events with similar audiences already exist and review their sponsor lists.

Once you have made all these calls, review your notes, and prepare a list of companies you will solicit. Yes, this takes a lot of time, but it can save your organization money. Instead of blindly sending out proposals to hundreds of businesses, ignoring their guidelines and focus areas, you can send dozens of proposals to companies who have already expressed interest in your event.

SEND PROPOSAL LETTERS.

It is important that sponsors feel you are asking for money specifically from their company, and they are not just part of a massive group.

Keep your letters short. As in your phone calls, concentrate on the exposure the company will receive for their money, not on how the money will help you. With large corporations, indeed, their marketing budgets are usually much larger than their charitable donations budget. You may come across a few companies that are not as interested in the publicity; they want to sponsor your event because they honestly believe in your organization's mission. They are an exceedingly rare—but much appreciated—bunch.

Whenever possible, customize the letter. A good attention-getter is attaching a post-it that says, "Thanks for speaking with me. Here's the information on our event." With the size and type of company in mind, request a particular level from each potential sponsor. Tell them the anticipated impressions such a sponsorship will yield. Impressions are calculated by finding the total number of times a sponsor's name will be seen or heard. For instance, say your event is expected to draw one hundred people. Your entrant-level sponsors might receive space to display a banner (100 impressions), their name announced twice (200 impressions), and their name in your organization's newsletter (350 impressions) and annual report (475 impressions), for a total of 1,125 impressions.

Make sure sponsor benefits are easily found in your letter and they are easy to understand. Consider using bullet points to make the benefits stand out. Make sure your letters include your name, address and phone number, the date and location of the event, and the address(es) to send checks and in-kind donations. If you have 501(c)(3) status, be sure to say so, as some companies will only sponsor those agencies. If your letter does not include a brief description (two paragraphs, or a few bullet points), of what your organization does, then include a one-page fact sheet or a tri-fold brochure on your organization. Hand signs each letter.

Finally, include a chart or brochure that details sponsor benefits at each level. If this is the second time your organization is hosting the event, include a flyer that lists the sponsors and describes the audience from the previous time.

FOLLOW UP.

Do not be afraid to call potential sponsors to find out their thoughts on sponsorship.

After receiving your letter, some companies will call you to say they are interested in sponsoring. Most will not. It is up to you to follow up with them for about two to three weeks after sending your proposal. Some people hesitate to follow up, thinking it will bother the company. Most large companies do not accept follow-up calls, so note that when you are making your initial call. But for those that do not mention "no follow-up," it is perfectly OK to do so. It is the best way to find out that an interested company did not receive your letter.

Some interested companies may request face-to-face meetings, but most sponsored communication will be done via phone, fax, and e-mail. One viable way to begin your follow-up call: "This is Such and Such from My Organization. I just wanted to follow up on the sponsorship request I sent. Do you have a few seconds?" If they do not, ask when a better time would be to call back. Then be sure to call back at the requested time. If they say yes, your response might be: "Do you have any questions? Does it look like something you might be interested in for this year?" If they are not interested, find out why not. Keep good notes so you remember next year not to re-call people who said they would not be interested. If they say yes, congratulations! You are on your way to building a strong list of sponsors.

CULTIVATE YOUR RELATIONSHIPS with sponsors.

Do not drop your sponsors once they have agreed to send you money.

One of the worst messages to send to a sponsor is: "I just cared about getting your money. Now that I've got it, I'm going to disappear." Make sure sponsors see that you value their support. Once a company has agreed to sponsor, send them a thank-you letter that recaps the benefits at the level they have chosen. After you receive their check, send another thank-you. If your organization has a newsletter, begin sending it to them. If you do not have a newsletter, send them periodic updates on your organization and/or the event. Any time you think a sponsor has a concern about something, give them a call. If a sponsor calls you, make it a point to return their call as soon as possible, and absolutely within 24 hours. If you will be out of the office for a few days, make sure your voice message directs sponsors to a live person.

CULTIVATE YOUR RELATIONSHIPS with non-sponsors.

People who were not able to sponsor may be interested in attending your event.

As your event draws near, send invitations to some of the companies that did not sponsor it. You might want to say something like, "Even though you weren't able to sponsor us this year, we hope you'll consider attending or volunteering during the event." Sometimes, an employee from the company will attend, see what a momentous event it is, and make sure money is budgeted next year for sponsorship.

GIVE YOUR SPONSORS plenty of publicity.

Publicity is why your sponsors signed on...so make sure they get it!

This sounds obvious, but make sure your sponsors receive everything promised. If you can give them added publicity, by way of a name announcement, etc., do so. You do not want to put all the work into acquiring sponsors and then not deliver results.

CULTIVATE RELATIONSHIPS with sponsors. Do not drop your sponsors after the event.

Send thank-you letters to sponsors after the event. Let them know how successful the event was, how much money was raised, the final attendance count, etc. For sponsors at elevated levels (or, if your event was exceedingly small, for all sponsors), put together packets that showcase their publicity. Include copies of all the ads they appeared in, photos of their banners at the event, photos of people using their products at the event, etc. If some sponsors had any concerns at any point, give them a call to see how they think things worked out. Even after the final tasks of the event have been taken care of, and that last thank-you has been sent, stay connected with your sponsors! Continue sending them your newsletter or updates on your group. Send them your annual report. Invite them to other events at your organization. Send them quick notes if you see their company given a positive mention in the newspaper. You do not want to only contact them once sponsorship solicitation starts up again. On the other hand, do not go overboard. For example, some sponsors prefer not to receive holiday cards from nonprofits, because they feel as though their money is not being spent in the best way. It can be a fine line, so use your judgment. The bottom line is recognizing that each sponsor has unique needs and concerns. Do what you can to accommodate your sponsors while striving to make your event a successful continuation of your organization's mission.

When the event is over, debrief (with yourself, if you did this alone; with your team if you had help). Make notes on what went well, and what did not. Think about refining your presentations and your event planning to build on what went well and avoid the bad bits.

Then, of course, do it all again for the next event.

Chapter 28

Build Your Email List

Email marketing is a high-impact, low-cost way of delivering your marketing message to current customers and prospects. Here are some ideas to build that email list.

1. Put out the sign-up sheet.

Whether you are at a trade show, community event or in your storefront, collecting email addresses in person can be as easy as putting out a signup sheet and encouraging people to write down their details.

2. Leverage business cards.

When you meet people face to face for any reason, ask for their business card. Offer yours. Set a glass bowl on the counter in your store or the reception desk in your office and ask visitors to drop their cards in it. Offer some incentive to do so — a free product or service, gift card, etc. Use your business cards to further drum up emails; add an offer on the back of your card that encourages people to sign up to receive your emails.

3. Host an event.

Stage an event — lunch gathering, topic talk, book club, or whatever works to get people in the door. Drop invitations at nearby businesses, post the notice on your front door and advertise in local media. Ask people to RSVP with their email addresses.

4. Invite people to 'join the club.'

Offer a birthday or anniversary club that allows people to "enroll" by providing their email address and relevant date. Reward them with an exclusive offer for signing up, and follow up with something else special, such as a discount coupon, on their birthday or anniversary date.

5. Organize a giveaway.

Using snail mail and/or your existing email list, send people a postcard asking for email information and offer them a reward for providing it.

6. Drum up emails with direct mail.

Sometimes you have a physical address but no email address. Send a direct mail offer they can only get by going to your website and joining your email list.

7. Try some telemarketing.

Throughout the day, you and your employees interact with many customers and prospects on the phone. Before you hang up, always ask if they would like to join your email list. Give them a brief statement of the benefits of enrolling — for example, exclusive offers and discounts only available to email subscribers.

8. Optimize your website for opt-ins.

If a customer or prospect visits your website, they are already at least interested. Do not miss the opportunity to add them to your email list. Include email registration forms on every main page of your site, as well as on the pages for popular products and services.

9. Build with your blog.

Your blog provides a wonderful way to build a personal relationship with customers and prospects — and to gather their email addresses. Consistently end blogs with a call to action that encourages readers to sign up for your email messages. Require blog visitors to provide an email list to leave comments and set it up so that they must actively opt out if they do not want their email address included on your mailing list.

10. Engage through social media.

Social media participation can allow you to reach new audiences and make new connections. Stay abreast of trending topics that are of interest to your customers and prospects. Use social media [1] to encourage people to visit one of the channels where they can sign up for your email list.

11. Do not give up on bounce-backs.

Everyone hates to see the dreaded bounce-back alert in their inbox. If you have snail-mail information to match an email address, send a postcard asking the contact to provide you with an updated email address so you can stay in touch. Consider rewarding them with a discount or freebie for taking the time to respond.

12. Piggyback on a colleague's efforts. Consider sharing email lists with neighbors.

businesses. Offer them space in your newsletter in exchange for including a link with your opt-in form in their newsletter.

---

1.   http://www.verticalresponse.com/blog/4-social-contests-that-help-you-grow-your-email-list-and-reach-new-people/

13. Do not let website visitors get away.

If a visitor gets through your entire website without opting in, grab them one last time before they go. Set a lightbox to appear asking for an email address whenever someone is about to navigate away from your website or blog.

14. Create an online community.

Platforms like WordPress make it easy to set up a community and foster interaction between your brand and your customers. Include a sign-up form for your newsletter on every page of the community.

15. Leverage 'email only' specials.

Reward your loyal email followers with specials that are only available to subscribers. Encourage them to forward the link to your sign-up page to friends and family.

16. Do not forget your email.

Be sure every email you send has an opt-in form so that anyone who receives one of your emails via forward from someone else, can sign up directly to be on your list.

17. Word of mouth still rocks.

Ask current and new customers to refer new subscribers to your list. Sweeten the deal by offering them a discount as a reward for valid, confirmed, and consent-backed email addresses.

18. Signs of the times.

Include a link to your opt-in page in the signature of all your emails, personal and professional.

19. Speak up for yourself.

Speaking engagements are a wonderful way to establish your company as active in the community, but you can also weave into your talk the idea that more information can be found on your website. Offer free consultations in exchange for signing up for your newsletter and emails.

20. Do not forget the power of print.

Add a QR code (a bar code that people can scan with a smartphone app) to print ads, direct-mail postcards, and other printed marketing materials. Use the code to allow people to opt-in to your email list simply by scanning the code.

Building an email list takes time and is critical to marketing success in the digital age.

Chapter 29

Web Site Marketing
1. Introduction

Web site marketing is a crucial aspect of any business's online presence. It involves the promotion and advertising of a company's website to attract and engage visitors. With the growing reliance on the internet, it has become essential for businesses to use effective marketing strategies to reach their target audience and stay competitive in the digital landscape. Through web site marketing, businesses can increase brand awareness, generate leads, drive traffic, and boost sales and revenue.

1.1. Importance of web site marketing

Web site marketing plays a significant role in the success of a business in today's digital age. It is essential because it helps businesses establish their online presence and reach a wider audience. By implementing effective web site marketing strategies, businesses can increase their visibility in search engine results, attract targeted traffic, and create meaningful connections with potential customers. Moreover, web site marketing allows businesses to stay competitive, build brand credibility, and establish themselves as industry leaders. It is a powerful tool that enables businesses to showcase their products/services, communicate their value proposition, and drive conversions.

1.2. Benefits of effective web site marketing

Implementing effective web site marketing strategies brings numerous benefits to businesses. Firstly, it helps in driving qualified traffic to the website, increasing the chances of converting visitors into customers. Secondly, web site marketing enables businesses to target specific demographics and geographic locations, ensuring that the marketing efforts are focused on the right audience. Additionally, effective web site marketing can enhance brand recognition and credibility, as well as foster customer loyalty and trust. Through regular monitoring and analysis of marketing efforts, businesses can also optimize their strategies for better results. Effective web site marketing leads to increased brand visibility, higher conversion rates, and improved business growth.

2. Strategies for web site marketing

Implementing effective strategies for web site marketing is crucial for businesses to attract and engage their target audience. This involves using.

various techniques and tactics to increase visibility and drive traffic to the website. Some key strategies include search engine optimization (SEO), social media marketing, content marketing, and pay-per-click (PPC) advertising. By combining these strategies, businesses can enhance their online presence, improve brand awareness, and boost conversions and revenue.

2.1. Search engine optimization (SEO)

Search engine optimization (SEO) is a fundamental strategy in web site marketing that focuses on improving a website's visibility and ranking in search engine results. Through optimizing website content, keywords, meta tags, and other factors, businesses can increase organic traffic and attract targeted visitors. SEO techniques include on-page optimization, link building, and technical optimization to ensure search engines can effectively crawl and index the website. By implementing SEO best practices, businesses can enhance their online visibility and improve their chances of reaching their target audience.

2.2. Social media marketing

Social media marketing is a powerful strategy for web site marketing that utilizes various social media platforms to connect with target audiences, build brand awareness, and drive website traffic. By creating engaging and shareable content, utilizing targeted advertising, and fostering conversations with followers, businesses can effectively promote their website and offerings. Social media marketing allows businesses to reach a wide audience, engage with potential customers, and build long-term relationships, leading to increased website traffic and conversions.

2.3. Content marketing

Content marketing is a strategy that involves creating and distributing valuable, relevant, and consistent content to attract and retain a clearly defined target audience. As part of web site marketing, content marketing aims to provide value to website visitors, establish the business as an industry authority, and drive conversions. By creating high-quality blog posts, articles, videos, infographics, and other types of content, businesses can position themselves as knowledgeable experts, thereby increasing website traffic and attracting a loyal audience.

2.4. Pay-per-click (PPC) advertising.

Pay-per-click (PPC) advertising is a form of online advertising where businesses pay each time a user clicks on their ads. This strategy allows businesses to bid on keywords relevant to their target audience, ensuring their ads appear in search engine results and on other platforms. PPC advertising can provide businesses with immediate visibility and targeted traffic to their website. With careful keyword selection, ad creation, and optimization, businesses can increase their website's visibility, generate leads, and drive conversions through PPC advertising.

3. Tools and techniques for web site marketing

To effectively market a website, various tools and techniques can be employed. These tools and techniques play a crucial role in analyzing, optimizing, and promoting a website's performance. By utilizing these tools, marketers can gain valuable insights into user behavior, track website traffic, and measure the success of marketing campaigns. Additionally, techniques such as conversion rate optimization and A/B testing allow for the testing and refinement of website elements to enhance user experience and increase conversion rates. Furthermore, influencer marketing and email marketing are powerful strategies to reach a wider audience and drive engagement with a website. Overall, these tools and techniques form the backbone of web site marketing and contribute to its effectiveness.

3.1. Google Analytics

Google Analytics is a widely used tool for web site marketing. It provides invaluable insights into website performance by tracking and analyzing user behavior. With Google Analytics, marketers can measure website traffic, understand audience demographics, track conversions, and identify the most popular pages on a website. This data helps in making informed decisions to optimize marketing strategies, improve user experience, and increase conversion rates. By utilizing the features and capabilities of Google Analytics, marketers can gain a deeper understanding of their website's performance and make data-driven decisions to enhance their web site marketing efforts.

3.2. Email marketing.

Email marketing is a powerful technique for web site marketing. By building a subscriber list and sending targeted emails, marketers can reach a wide audience directly in their inboxes. Email marketing allows for personalized communication, enabling marketers to tailor their messages to different segments of their audience. This technique is effective for promoting products, services, blog posts, or any other content related to the website. Additionally, by analyzing open rates, click-through rates, and conversion rates from email campaigns, marketers can gain insights into user engagement and refine their email marketing strategies for greater effectiveness. With the proper implementation of email marketing, websites can not only drive traffic but also generate leads and conversions.

3.3. Conversion rate optimization (CRO)

Conversion rate optimization (CRO) focuses on improving the percentage of website visitors who take a desired action, such as making a purchase, signing up for a newsletter, or completing a form. By conducting thorough analysis, marketers can identify barriers to conversion and implement strategies to overcome them. This involves optimizing website design, improving call-to-action elements, streamlining the checkout process, and enhancing overall user experience. With CRO techniques in place, marketers can increase the effectiveness of their web site marketing efforts by maximizing the conversion potential from existing website traffic.

3.4. A/B testing

A/B testing is a technique used in web site marketing to compare two versions of a webpage or element to determine which one performs better. By splitting website traffic between the two variations and measuring metrics such as conversion rates or click-through rates, marketers can gather data to make informed decisions about which version is more effective. This allows for the identification of elements that resonate better with users and can lead to improved website performance. A/B testing is an ongoing process that helps marketers optimize their websites and deliver a better user experience, resulting in increased engagement and conversions.

3.5. Influencer marketing

Influencer marketing leverages the popularity and credibility of influential individuals in a specific niche to promote a website or its products/services. By collaborating with influencers who have a strong following and align with the website's target audience, marketers can tap into their reach and reputation to increase brand visibility and drive traffic. Influencers can create sponsored content, provide reviews, or endorse the website, thereby influencing their followers to visit and engage with the website. This form of marketing can be highly effective in reaching a wider audience and establishing trust, credibility, and authenticity for the website and its offerings.

4. Best practices for web site marketing

Implementing best practices for web site marketing can significantly improve the effectiveness of your online presence. By following these practices, you can ensure that your website is optimized for search engines, engaging your target audience, and effectively promoting your products or services. Best practices include conducting thorough target audience research, creating compelling and valuable content, building a strong online presence across various platforms, monitoring and

analyzing performance metrics, and continuously adapting and improving your marketing strategies.

4.1. Target audience research

Target audience research is a crucial step in successful web site marketing. It involves gathering information about the demographics, preferences, and behavior of your potential customers. By understanding your target audience, you can tailor your marketing strategies to effectively reach and engage them. Research methods may include surveys, interviews, and analysis of website analytics. This information allows you to create relevant and targeted content, choose appropriate marketing channels, and develop personalized strategies to attract and retain your desired audience.

4.2. Creating compelling content

Creating compelling content is essential for capturing and retaining the attention of your target audience. High-quality content that is informative, engaging, and valuable can establish your website as a trusted resource in your industry. It should be tailored to the needs and interests of your target audience, using language and tone that resonates with them. Compelling content can take the form of blog posts, articles, videos, infographics, and more. By consistently delivering valuable content, you can increase brand awareness, attract organic traffic, and encourage audience engagement.

4.3. Building a strong online presence

Building a strong online presence is crucial for effective web site marketing. This involves establishing your brand across various digital platforms such as social media, search engines, and industry-specific directories. Consistent branding, including your logo, colors, and messaging, helps build recognition and credibility. Engaging with your audience through social media, responding to comments, and participating in relevant online communities can also enhance your online presence. Additionally, optimizing your website for search engines and implementing search engine optimization (SEO) techniques can improve your visibility in search results, driving more organic traffic to your site.

4.4. Monitoring and analyzing performance.

Monitoring and analyzing the performance of your website marketing efforts is crucial for evaluating the effectiveness of your strategies and making data-driven decisions. By using tools like Google Analytics, you can track key metrics such as website traffic, conversion rates, and user engagement. This data provides insights into which marketing campaigns are driving results and helps identify areas for

improvement. By continuously monitoring performance, you can optimize your marketing efforts, allocate resources effectively, and make informed decisions to achieve your goals.

4.5. Continuous improvement and adaptation

Continuous improvement and adaptation are key principles in successful web site marketing. The digital landscape is constantly evolving, and it is crucial to regularly evaluate and adjust your strategies to stay ahead of the competition. By analyzing performance metrics, user feedback, and market trends, you can identify areas for improvement and make necessary adjustments to your website design, content, and marketing campaigns. Adapting to changes in consumer behavior, emerging technologies, and industry trends allows you to remain relevant and responsive, ensuring your web site marketing efforts continue to generate positive results.

Chapter 30

How To Make Your Video Trend

1. Make your video easy to find

One of the key factors in making your video easy to find is optimizing your video title. A catchy and descriptive title can attract viewers' attention and make them more likely to click on your video. Additionally, using relevant tags is essential in improving discoverability. Tags help search engines and platforms categorize your video, making it more likely to appear in relevant searches. Another important aspect is including keywords in the video description. By using relevant keywords that describe your video, you increase the chances of it being found by users looking for content like yours. Lastly, utilizing hashtags can also be effective in increasing the visibility of your video. By adding relevant and popular hashtags, your video can be discovered by users browsing videos with similar themes or topics.

1.1. Optimize your video title.

An optimized video title plays a crucial role in making your video easy to find. It should be concise, yet descriptive, giving a clear idea of what the video is about. Including keywords related to the content of your video can help it appear in search results. Additionally, using attention-grabbing words or phrases can make your title more compelling and increase the likelihood of viewers clicking on your video.

1.2. Use relevant tags.

Using relevant tags is an effective way to make your video more discoverable. When choosing tags for your video, consider the keywords that are relevant to the content and theme of your video. You can also analyze the tags used by other popular videos in your niche to get inspiration. Including a mix of broad and specific tags can help your video reach a wider audience while still targeting specific viewers interested in your content.

1.3. Include keywords in the video description.

When writing the video description, it is important to include keywords that are relevant to the content and subject of your video. This helps search engines and platforms understand what your video is about, making it more likely to appear in relevant search results. However, avoid keyword stuffing and make sure the description reads naturally and provides valuable information to viewers. A well-crafted video description can increase the chances of your video being discovered and watched.

1.4. Utilize hashtags.

Utilizing hashtags in your video can help improve its visibility and reach. Hashtags allow your video to be grouped with other videos that have similar themes or topics, making it easier for users to discover your content. When choosing hashtags, opt for relevant and popular ones that are commonly used in your niche. This increases the likelihood of your video being seen by users who are actively searching or browsing videos with those hashtags. Simply adding a few well-chosen hashtags can significantly enhance the visibility of your video.

2. Make your video interesting to watch

One of the key factors in making your video trend is to make it interesting to watch. The more engaging and compelling your video is, the more likely it will capture the attention of viewers and keep them watching until the end. By creating content that is unique, entertaining, and informative, you can increase the chances of your video going viral. Whether it is showcasing a unique talent, sharing a funny story, or providing valuable tips, make sure your video offers something that viewers cannot resist.

2.1. Create engaging content.

Creating engaging content is crucial when it comes to making your video trend. To keep viewers interested and invested in your video, it is important to captivate their attention from the start. Start your video with a captivating hook that grabs the viewer's interest right away. Whether it is a surprising fact, a compelling question, or an exciting visual, make sure it piques their curiosity. Additionally, storytelling is a powerful tool to engage viewers. Structure your video in a way that has a clear beginning, middle, and end, and use storytelling techniques to create suspense and emotional connection with your audience.

2.2. Use high-quality visuals and audio.

High-quality visuals and audio play a significant role in making your video interesting to watch. Ensure that your video is visually appealing by using high-resolution footage, well-composed shots, and visually engaging graphics or animations. If you are using text or captions, make sure they are easy to read and visually appealing as well. Moreover, pay attention to the audio quality of your video. Use clear and crisp sound and consider adding background music or sound effects to enhance the overall viewing experience. Poor visuals or audio can distract viewers and diminish their interest in your video.

2.3. Keep the video concise and to the point.

Keeping your video concise and to the point is essential for maintaining viewers' interest and increasing the likelihood of it trending. In today's fast-paced digital world, people have shorter attention spans, so it is crucial to deliver your message efficiently. Identify the core message or purpose of your video and focus on conveying it concisely. Remove any unnecessary or repetitive content that could cause viewers to lose interest. Aim for a video length that is appropriate for your topic and target audience, typically ranging from a few minutes to around ten minutes. By keeping your video concise and focused, you will maximize its impact and engagement.

3. Attract plenty of viewers

To attract plenty of viewers to your video, you need to utilize various strategies. One effective way is to promote your video on social media platforms. By sharing your video on platforms like Facebook, Instagram, and Twitter, you can reach a wider audience and increase the chances of your video being seen. Another method is to collaborate with influencers or other creators in your niche. Partnering with popular personalities can help you tap into their existing fan base and gain more exposure for your video. Additionally, it is important to utilize SEO techniques to improve the visibility of your video. This includes optimizing your video title, using relevant tags, and incorporating keywords in the video description. Lastly, sharing your video on relevant online communities can also attract viewers who are interested in the topic of your video.

3.1. Promote your video on social media.

Promoting your video on social media is essential to attract viewers and make it trend. Utilize popular social media platforms such as Facebook, Instagram, and Twitter to share your video with your followers and engage with a wider audience. Create eye-catching posts with enticing captions and thumbnails that encourage people to click and watch your video. You can also make use of hashtags related to your video's topic to increase its discoverability. Engage with your audience by responding to comments and encouraging them to share your video with their friends and followers. By actively promoting your video on social media, you can increase its visibility and attract more viewers.

3.2. Collaborate with influencers or other creators.

Collaborating with influencers or other creators in your niche can significantly boost the visibility of your video and attract more viewers. Identify influencers or creators who have a large following and are relevant to your video's topic. Reach out to them and propose a collaboration where both parties can benefit. This could involve

featuring them in your video or vice versa, or simply cross promoting each other's content. By leveraging the existing fan base of influencers or creators, you can tap into a wider audience and increase the chances of your video being shared and trending. Collaborations not only help in attracting viewers but also foster valuable connections within your industry.

3.3. Utilize SEO techniques to improve visibility.

To improve the visibility of your video and attract more viewers, it is important to utilize SEO techniques. Start by optimizing your video title with keywords that accurately describe the content.

Additionally, make use of relevant tags that represent the key topics or themes of your video. This will help search engines and video platforms better understand and categorize your video. Incorporate keywords organically in the video description while providing a concise and informative summary. By following SEO best practices, you can increase the chances of your video appearing in search results and suggested video sections, attracting more viewers.

3.4. Share your video on relevant online communities.

Sharing your video on relevant online communities can be an effective way to attract viewers and increase its visibility. Identify online communities or forums that focus on topics related to your video and actively engage with the community members. Share your video within the community while providing a brief explanation or summary. Ensure your video aligns with the community guidelines to avoid any negative reactions. Actively participate in discussions and respond to comments to foster engagement and build relationships with the community members. By sharing your video in relevant online communities, you can reach an audience that already has an interest in the topic, increasing the likelihood of attracting more viewers.

4. Get viewers to share your video

After putting in the effort to create an amazing video, you will want to make sure it gets shared as much as possible. To encourage viewers to share your video, there are several strategies you can use. Firstly, include a call-to-action in your video, asking viewers to share it with their friends and followers. This can be as simple as saying, "If you enjoyed this video, please share it!" Secondly, encourage viewers to like, comment, and subscribe to your channel. This engagement not only increases visibility but also makes it more likely for viewers to share the video. Finally, offer incentives for sharing, such as giveaways or discounts. People are more likely to share content if they have something to gain, so consider rewarding those who help spread the word about your video.

4.1. Include a call-to-action in your video.

When it comes to getting your video shared, one effective strategy is to include a call-to-action. A call-to-action is a clear instruction to the viewer, motivating them to take a specific action. In this case, you want them to share your video. To incorporate a call-to-action in your video, you can simply ask viewers to share it with others or provide a direct link to share on social media platforms. You can also add text overlays or annotations that encourage sharing. By including a clear call-to-action, you are reminding viewers to share your video and increasing the likelihood that they will take that action.

4.2. Encourage viewers to like, comment, and subscribe.

To maximize the potential for your video to be shared, it is important to engage with your viewers and encourage them to like, comment, and subscribe to your channel. By building a dedicated community of viewers, you increase the chances of getting your video shared. To encourage these actions, be sure to ask viewers to like, comment, and subscribe throughout your video. Remind them why it is important and how it helps support your channel. Additionally, interact with the comments section and respond to comments as much as possible. By fostering a sense of community and actively engaging with your viewers, you create a positive environment that encourages sharing and further engagement with your content.

4.3. Offer incentives for sharing, such as giveaways or discounts.

If you want to motivate viewers to share your video, offering incentives can be a powerful strategy. One way to do this is by organizing giveaways or contests where viewers can enter to win prizes. By sharing the video, viewers gain an entry or increase their chances of winning. This creates a sense of excitement and encourages sharing among your audience. Another approach is to offer exclusive discounts or special promotions to viewers who share your video. This not only gives them a reason to share, but also provides value to those who engage with your content. By providing incentives, you give viewers a reward for their support and encourage them to share your video with others.

Chapter 31

How to Promote Your Website Free

1. Social Media Promotion

One effective way to promote your website for free is through social media. By leveraging platforms such as Facebook, Twitter, and Instagram, you can reach a large audience and increase your website traffic. To make your social media promotion successful, it is essential to create engaging content that captivates your audience. This can include informative posts, entertaining videos, or visually appealing images. Additionally, using relevant hashtags in your social media posts can help increase your visibility and attract a wider audience who are searching for specific topics. Collaborating with influencers who have a strong following in your niche can also be beneficial, as they can help amplify your reach and introduce your website to their audience. Lastly, running contests and giveaways can generate excitement and encourage people to visit your website and engage with your content.

1.1. Create engaging content.

Creating engaging content is crucial when promoting your website for free. High-quality and captivating content will not only attract visitors but also keep them coming back for more. To create engaging content, focus on providing value to your audience by offering useful information or solving their problems. This can be achieved through well-researched articles, informative videos, or entertaining blog posts. Incorporate storytelling techniques to make your content more relatable and memorable. Consider using visual elements such as images, infographics, or videos to enhance engagement. Remember to keep your content consistent and aligned with your brand's voice and values.

1.2. Use relevant hashtags.

Using relevant hashtags in your social media posts can significantly boost the visibility of your website and attract a larger audience. Hashtags help categorize and organize content, making it easier for users to discover your posts when searching for specific topics. Research and identify the most popular and relevant hashtags within your industry or niche. Mix popular and niche-specific hashtags to increase the chances of reaching a broader audience while still targeting your desired demographic. However, avoid using too many hashtags, as it can make your content appear spammy or desperate for attention. Aim for a balance, and monitor the performance of different hashtags to determine which ones are most effective for your website promotion.

1.3. Collaborate with influencers.

Collaborating with influencers who have established credibility in your industry or niche can benefit your website promotion. Influencers often have a loyal and engaged following who trust their recommendations. By partnering with influencers, you can leverage their influence to introduce your website to their audience. Seek out influencers whose values and target audience align with your own. This ensures that their followers are more likely to be interested in your website and offerings. Whether it is through sponsored posts, guest blogging, or hosting joint live sessions, collaborating with influencers can significantly increase your website's visibility and drive organic traffic.

1.4. Run contests and giveaways.

Running contests and giveaways is an effective strategy to promote your website and engage your audience. People love the chance to win prizes, and by hosting a contest or giveaway, you can incentivize them to visit your website, explore your content, and share it with others. Choose prizes that are relevant to your target audience and align with your website's offerings. This ensures that the participants are genuinely interested in your website and more likely to convert into regular visitors or customers. Encourage participants to share the contest or giveaway on social media platforms to expand your reach. This word-of-mouth marketing can generate buzz and attract new visitors to your website.

2. Search Engine Optimization (SEO)

Search Engine Optimization (SEO) is a crucial aspect of promoting your website for free. By optimizing your website for search engines, you can improve its visibility and increase organic traffic. There are several strategies to implement SEO effectively. Some of these include conducting keyword research, optimizing meta tags and descriptions, and improving website loading speed. By incorporating these techniques, you can enhance your website's ranking on search engine results pages, making it easier for users to find and navigate your site.

2.1. Conduct keyword research.

Conducting keyword research is an essential step in optimizing your website for search engines. By identifying relevant and high-traffic keywords that align with your website's content, you can improve its visibility on search engine results pages. Start by researching popular search terms related to your industry or niche using tools like Google Keyword Planner or SEMrush. Focus on long-tail keywords, which are more specific and have less competition. Incorporate these keywords naturally into your website's content, including headings, subheadings, and body text, to boost your chances of ranking higher in search results.

2.2. Optimize meta tags and descriptions.

Optimizing meta tags and descriptions is another important aspect of SEO. Meta tags provide information about your web page to search engines, while meta descriptions give users a summary of what to expect when they click on your website. Make sure to include relevant keywords in your title tags and meta descriptions to increase your website's visibility on search engine results pages. Additionally, write compelling and concise meta descriptions that entice users to click through to your site. By optimizing these elements, you can improve your website's click-through rate and attract more organic traffic.

2.3. Improve website loading speed.

Improving website loading speed is crucial for both user experience and SEO. Slow-loading websites can lead to higher bounce rates, as users tend to leave if a site takes too long to load. This can negatively impact your website's rankings on search engine results pages. To improve website loading speed, consider optimizing your images by compressing them and using asynchronous loading for scripts. Minimize HTTP requests by combining CSS and JavaScript files. Utilize browser caching to reduce the load time for returning visitors. By implementing these strategies, you can enhance your website's performance, provide a better user experience, and increase your chances of ranking higher in search engine results.

3. Content Marketing

Content marketing is a powerful strategy to promote your website and attract more visitors. By consistently creating informative and valuable content, you can establish yourself as an authority in your industry and drive organic traffic to your site. There are various tactics you can employ to effectively execute content marketing. These include writing informative blog posts, guest posting on other websites, creating shareable infographics, producing engaging videos, and offering free downloadable resources. By implementing these strategies, you can provide valuable information to your target audience and increase the visibility of your website.

3.1. Write informative blog posts.

One of the key components of content marketing is writing informative blog posts. By regularly publishing high-quality blog articles that offer valuable insights, tips, and advice related to your industry, you can attract and engage your target audience. Ensure that the content is well-researched, engaging, and addresses the pain points of your readers. Incorporate relevant keywords naturally throughout the blog post to optimize it for search engines. By consistently creating informative blog posts, you can establish your expertise, build trust with your audience, and drive more traffic to your website.

3.2. Guest post on other websites

Guest posting on other websites is an effective way to expand your reach and promote your website. Look for reputable websites in your niche that accept guest contributions and offer to author informative articles for them. Make sure the content you provide is valuable and relevant to their audience. Include a compelling bio or author box that directs readers back to your website. By guest posting, you can tap into the existing audience of the host website and increase your visibility. It also helps in building relationships with other industry experts and influencers.

3.3. Create shareable infographics.

Infographics are visually appealing and highly shareable content pieces that can generate significant traffic to your website. Create informative and visually appealing infographics that present data, statistics, or tips in a visually engaging format. Make sure the information you provide is valuable and relevant to your target audience. Optimize the infographic with your website's branding and include social sharing buttons to encourage readers to share it on their social media platforms. By creating shareable infographics, you can attract attention, increase your website's reach, and drive more traffic.

3.4. Produce engaging videos.

Videos have gained immense popularity in recent years and can be a powerful tool to promote your website. Produce engaging videos that provide valuable information, showcase your products or services, or offer tutorials related to your industry. Optimize the videos for search engines by incorporating relevant keywords in titles, descriptions, and tags. Publish the videos on platforms like YouTube and embed them on your website to increase visibility. Engaging videos can capture the attention of your target audience, increase engagement, and drive traffic to your website.

3.5. Offer free downloadable resources.

Providing free downloadable resources is a strategy that can attract visitors to your website and establish your authority in your industry. Create valuable resources such as eBooks, guides, templates, or checklists that address the pain points or challenges faced by your target audience. Offer these resources as free downloads on your website in exchange for visitors providing their email addresses. This

allows you to build a valuable email list and nurture leads. By offering free downloadable resources, you can position yourself as a trusted source of information and attract potential customers to your website.

4. Networking and Collaboration

Networking and collaboration are essential for promoting your website. By connecting with others in your industry, you can expand your reach and visibility. There are several ways to do this effectively. You can join online communities and forums related to your niche. Engage in discussions, share your expertise, and build relationships with like-minded individuals. Collaborating with complementary businesses is another wonderful way to increase your website's exposure. Look for companies that offer products or services that complement yours and find ways to work together. This can include exchanging guest posts, cross-promoting each other on social media, or even creating joint marketing campaigns. Lastly, attending industry events and conferences gives you the opportunity to meet influencers, potential customers, and industry experts. Make sure to network, exchange contact information, and promote your website during these events. Overall, networking and collaboration can significantly boost your website's visibility and help you reach a wider audience.

4.1. Join online communities and forums.

Joining online communities and forums is an effective way to promote your website for free. Look for platforms and forums that are relevant to your industry or niche. Participate in discussions, answer questions, and share valuable insights to establish yourself as an expert in your field. By actively engaging with the community, you can build trust and credibility, leading to increased visibility for your website. Additionally, you can include a link to your website in your forum signature or profile, driving traffic directly to your site. Remember to abide by the rules and guidelines of each community, and always provide helpful and relevant contributions. This way, you can leverage the power of online communities and forums to attract more visitors to your website.

4.2. Collaborate with complementary businesses.

Collaborating with complementary businesses can be a mutually beneficial way to promote your website and reach a wider audience. Identify businesses that offer products or services that complement yours without direct competition. For example, if you sell workout equipment, you could collaborate with a fitness trainer or a nutritionist. By combining your expertise and resources, you can create joint content, such as guest blog posts or video tutorials, which appeal to both of your target audiences. Additionally, you can cross-promote each other through social media shoutouts, featuring each other's products or services, or offering exclusive discounts to each other's customers. These collaborations not only expand your reach but also introduce you to new potential customers who may have a genuine interest in what your website has to offer.

4.3. Attending industry events and conferences.

Attending industry events and conferences provides an excellent opportunity to promote your website and connect with key individuals in your field. These events gather industry experts, influencers, and potential customers under one roof. It is important to prepare before attending by creating business cards with your website and contact information. During the event, try to network with other attendees, exchange ideas, and showcase your website. Engage in conversations, share your expertise, and listen to what others have to say. Consider participating as a speaker or panelist to further establish yourself as an authority in your industry. Remember to follow up with the people you meet after the event, connecting with them on social media and continuing the conversation. By taking advantage of industry events and conferences, you can raise awareness of your website and build valuable connections that can lead to increased traffic and opportunities.

Chapter 32

Increase Web Traffic via Real World Promotion!

1. Introduction

Increasing web traffic is crucial for the success of any online business. With the ever-growing number of websites and online platforms, competition for audience attention is fierce. This is where real world promotion comes into play. By combining offline advertising, event sponsorship and participation, and utilizing physical locations, businesses can effectively drive more traffic to their websites. In this guide, we will explore various strategies and techniques to help you increase web traffic through real world promotion.

1.1. The Importance of Web Traffic

Web traffic is the lifeblood of any website or online business. It refers to the number of visitors and the amount of data they generate by accessing web pages. The importance of web traffic lies in its direct correlation with success and profitability. More traffic means more potential customers, leads, and conversions. It also enhances brand visibility and online presence. Without a steady stream of web traffic, a website may struggle to achieve its goals and objectives. Therefore, understanding the significance of web traffic is essential for any business aiming for online success.

1.2. Real World Promotion as a Strategy

Real world promotion, also known as offline marketing, involves utilizing traditional advertising and promotional methods to drive traffic to a website. It complements online marketing efforts and enables businesses to reach a wider audience beyond the digital sphere. Real world promotion includes strategies such as offline advertising, event sponsorship and participation, and utilizing physical locations. By incorporating these strategies into your marketing mix, you can expand your reach, enhance brand recognition, and increase web traffic. In the following sections, we will delve deeper into these strategies and explore their effectiveness in driving online traffic.

2. Section 1: Offline Advertising

Offline advertising is a valuable strategy to increase web traffic and reach a wider audience. By utilizing traditional advertising methods in the real world, businesses can generate more attention and drive traffic to their websites. There are various offline advertising techniques that can be employed, including billboards and outdoor ads, print advertising in newspapers and magazines, and flyers and brochures distribution. Each of these methods has its own benefits and can be used strategically to target specific demographics. By incorporating offline advertising into your marketing efforts, you can effectively promote your website and attract more visitors.

2.1. Billboards and Outdoor Ads

Billboards and outdoor ads are powerful tools for increasing web traffic. Placing

Eye-catching advertisements in high-traffic areas can grab the attention of passersby and encourage them to visit your website. These large displays allow you to showcase your brand and message in a visually appealing and memorable way. With strategic placement and compelling content, billboards and outdoor ads can effectively drive traffic to your website. By targeting specific locations and demographics, you can maximize the impact of this offline advertising method and reach a wider audience.

2.2. Print Advertising in Newspapers and Magazines

Print advertising in newspapers and magazines remains an effective way to increase web traffic. Many people still enjoy reading physical publications, and placing advertisements in these mediums allows you to reach potential customers who may not be active online. By crafting compelling ads with clear calls to action, you can encourage readers to visit your website and explore what you have to offer. Additionally, print ads in niche or local publications can specifically target relevant audiences, increasing the chances of driving qualified traffic to your website. Incorporating print advertising into your marketing mix can help you expand your online presence and attract more visitors.

2.3. Flyers and Brochures Distribution

Flyers and brochures distribution is a cost-effective offline advertising strategy that can effectively drive web traffic. By creating visually appealing materials with enticing offers or information about your products or services, you can quickly grab the attention of potential customers. Distributing these materials in high-traffic areas, such as shopping centers, libraries, or community notice boards, can broaden your reach and generate interest in your website. Additionally, including QR codes or website URLs on your flyers and brochures makes it easy for recipients to directly access your website. This offline advertising method allows you to target specific geographic areas and engage with local communities, increasing your web traffic.

3. Event Sponsorship and Participation

Event sponsorship and participation can be a powerful way to increase web traffic. By sponsoring local events, you can not only gain visibility but also build strong relationships with the community. Sponsoring events allows you to showcase your brand to a targeted audience, which can lead to increased website visits. Additionally, hosting workshops or seminars gives you the opportunity to position yourself as an expert in your industry and attract potential customers who are interested in your products or services. Attending trade shows and conferences provides another avenue to connect with your target market and generate buzz around your website. Collaborating with influencers or local celebrities further amplifies your reach and helps to drive traffic to your website. By leveraging real-world events and partnerships, you can effectively promote your website and attract a larger audience.

3.1. Sponsoring Local Events

Sponsoring local events can significantly boost web traffic. When you sponsor local events, your brand gains exposure to a captive audience. This exposure can lead to a surge in website visitors who are interested in the event and are likely to explore your offerings. By aligning your brand with local events that resonate with your target audience, you can effectively drive traffic to your website. Sponsoring local events not only increases your visibility but also establishes your brand as a supportive and involved member of the community. This positive association can translate into increased website visits and customer loyalty.

3.2. Hosting Workshops or Seminars

Hosting workshops or seminars is a strategic way to increase web traffic. By positioning yourself as an expert in your field and sharing valuable knowledge, you can attract individuals who are interested in your expertise and offerings. Workshops and seminars provide an opportunity to engage with potential customers directly, build trust and credibility, and drive traffic to your website. By offering valuable insights and actionable advice during these events, you can pique attendees' interest and encourage them to visit your website for more information, resources, and opportunities for further engagement.

3.3. Attending Trade Shows and Conferences

Attending trade shows and conferences is a smart strategy to increase web traffic. These events gather professionals and enthusiasts from your industry in one place, offering a prime opportunity to showcase your brand and attract potential customers. By setting up a well-designed booth, engaging with attendees, and providing informative materials, you can capture interest and encourage individuals to visit your website. Trade shows and conferences also allow you to stay updated on industry trends, connect with like-minded professionals, and foster valuable relationships that can contribute to increased website traffic through referrals and collaborations.

3.4. Collaborating with Influencers or Local Celebrities

Collaborating with influencers or local celebrities can be a meaningful change in boosting web traffic. These individuals have a dedicated following and can greatly influence their audience's decisions. By partnering with relevant influencers or local celebrities who align with your brand values, you can tap into their existing fan base and redirect them to your website. Collaborations can take the form of sponsored content, product reviews, giveaways, or joint promotions. This mutually beneficial partnership expands your reach, exposes your brand to a wider audience, and drives traffic to your website. Leveraging the influence and popularity of influencers and local celebrities can significantly increase your web traffic and enhance brand awareness.

4. Section 3: Utilizing Physical Locations

Utilizing physical locations can boost web traffic for your business. By strategically placing window displays and signage in high-traffic areas, you can catch the attention of passing pedestrians and potential customers. These displays can showcase your products or services, enticing people to visit your website. Additionally, vehicle wraps and decals are an effective way to promote your website while on the move. With eye-catching designs and your web address prominently displayed on your vehicle, you can generate interest and curiosity from fellow drivers and pedestrians. Branded merchandise and giveaways also serve as an indirect way to promote your website. By distributing items such as pens, t-shirts, or mugs with your website URL, you create tangible reminders of your online presence that customers can take home with them. All these real-world promotion tactics can drive web traffic by increasing brand visibility and piquing curiosity.

4.1. Window Displays and Signage

Window displays and signage are powerful tools for increasing web traffic. By creating visually appealing and engaging window displays, you can grab the attention of passersby and draw them into your store. By prominently displaying your website URL on these displays, you can encourage potential customers to visit your site for more information or to make a purchase. Similarly, signage placed strategically around your physical location can serve as a constant reminder of your online presence. It is important to design these displays and signage with clarity and creativity to make them stand out and create an impression. With the right combination of attractive visuals and clear website information, window displays, and signage can effectively drive web traffic.

4.2. Vehicle Wraps and Decals

Vehicle wraps and decals offer a unique and attention-grabbing way to increase web traffic. By adorning your company vehicles with eye-catching designs that prominently feature your website URL, you can create mobile advertisements that reach a wide audience. These moving billboards capture the attention of fellow drivers and pedestrians, arousing curiosity and prompting them to visit your website. Whether your vehicles are parked or on the road, they serve as a constant advertisement for your online presence. This form of real-world promotion can be particularly effective in densely populated areas or during events where there is a high concentration of people. Investing in vehicle wraps and decals is a smart way to maximize your brand exposure and boost web traffic.

4.3. Branded Merchandise and Giveaways

Branded merchandise and giveaways are an excellent way to promote your website and drive web traffic. By offering items such as pens, t-shirts, or keychains with your website URL, you create a tangible connection between your brand and the target audience. These items act as constant reminders of your online presence, as customers can use them in their daily lives. When distributing these branded products, it is important to choose high-quality items that align with your brand image. The more useful and desirable the merchandise, the more likely it is to be kept and used, exposing your website to a wider audience. Additionally, hosting contests or giveaways where participants must visit your website to enter can generate immediate traffic and engagement. By incorporating branded merchandise and giveaways into your marketing strategy, you can effectively increase web traffic and generate awareness for your brand.

Chapter 33

How to Make a No-Budget Music Video

1. Planning Your Video

Planning your music video is an essential step to ensure a smooth production process. Start by considering the overall concept and message you want to convey through the video. This will help you choose a suitable song that aligns with your vision. Next, brainstorm different video ideas that can complement the lyrics and mood of the song. Once you have an unobstructed vision, create a storyboard that outlines the sequence of shots and scenes you want to capture. Finally, find suitable shooting locations that will enhance the visual appeal of your video.

1.1. Choose a Song

Choosing the right song for your no-budget music video is crucial. Look for songs that resonate with your personal style and genre. Consider the tempo, lyrics, and overall mood of the song to ensure it aligns with your desired video concept. It is also important to choose a song that you have the necessary rights or permissions to use for your video. Select a song that allows you the creative freedom to visualize and bring your ideas to life without any legal complications.

1.2. Brainstorm Video Ideas

Brainstorming video ideas is an exciting part of the creative process. Start by listening to the chosen song and jotting down any visual ideas or themes that come to mind. Consider the emotions evoked by the music and how you can capture them visually. Explore different concepts, settings, and narratives that can enhance the viewer's experience. Do not be afraid to think freely and experiment with unconventional ideas. The goal is to generate a range of potential concepts for your music video.

1.3. Create a Storyboard

Creating a storyboard is an essential step in planning your no-budget music video. A storyboard is a visual representation that breaks down each scene into individual shots. Sketch out each shot, including details such as camera angles, movements, and composition. It helps you organize your ideas, ensure a coherent storyline, and communicate your vision to the team involved. Consider the flow of the video and how each shot transitions to the next. This will serve as a helpful roadmap during the filming and editing stages.

1.4. Find Locations for Shooting

Finding suitable locations for shooting is crucial to enhance the visual appeal of your music video. Look for locations that complement the overall concept and mood of the song. Consider both indoor and outdoor options, such as parks, abandoned buildings, or unique spaces that align with your artistic vision. Keep in mind the coordination of shooting in each location, including any necessary permissions or restrictions. Explore your local community for potential free or low-cost locations that add depth and interest to your video.

2. GATHERING EQUIPMENT and Props

When creating a no-budget music video, gathering equipment and props can be a bit challenging. However, it is possible. In this section, we will explore many ways to acquire the necessary items without breaking the bank. From using what you already have at your disposal to borrowing or renting equipment, we will provide you with practical tips to ensure you have everything you need to bring your vision to life. Additionally, we will discuss how to get creative with props, offering innovative ideas to make your video visually captivating without spending a fortune.

2.1. Use What You Already Have

One of the most cost-effective ways to gather equipment and props for your no-budget music video is to utilize what you already have. Look around your house or the spaces where you will be shooting the video. Think about objects that can be repurposed or creatively used to enhance the visual narrative. For example, your old lamps can be used to create interesting lighting effects, while your collection of vintage clothes can be used as costumes. Do not underestimate the power of resourcefulness when it comes to making the most out of the objects you already own.

2.2. Borrow or Rent Equipment

If you find yourself in need of specific equipment that you do not already have, consider borrowing or renting it. Reach out to friends, family, or fellow musicians who may have the gear you require. People are often willing to lend a hand, especially if they believe in your musical project. Additionally, look for local community centers or music stores that offer equipment rentals at affordable rates. By exploring these options, you can save money and still have access to the necessary equipment to produce your no-budget music video.

2.3. Get Creative with Props

Props play a crucial role in bringing your music video to life, even on a no-budget production. Instead of spending money on expensive props, get creative and think freely. Look for everyday objects that can be repurposed to fit the theme or mood of your video. A simple cardboard box can become a spaceship, or a vintage suitcase can add a touch of nostalgia. Do not be afraid to experiment and think freely when it comes to choosing and using props. With a little bit of imagination, you can create visually stunning scenes without spending a dime.

3. Filming the Video

Once you have planned your video and gathered all the necessary equipment and props, it is time to start filming. This section will guide you through the process of shooting your no-budget music video. The key is to be creative and make the most of what you have. Remember, you do not need fancy cameras or a big production crew to create something special. With some ingenuity and a bit of collaboration, you can capture amazing footage for your music video.

3.1. Recruit Friends as Actors

One of the best ways to save money on actors is to recruit your friends. Ask around and see if any of your friends are interested in being a part of your music video. Not only will this help you cut costs, but it also adds a delicate touch to your video. Your friends will be more comfortable in front of the camera, which can translate to more natural and authentic performances. So do not be afraid to reach out and involve your friends in your creative project!

3.2. Use Natural Lighting

Lighting is key in any video production, and when you are working with a no-budget, it is important to make the most of natural lighting. Shoot your video during the day and take advantage of the sunlight. Position your subjects and the camera in a way that utilizes the natural light to create interesting and dynamic visuals. You can experiment with the angle and intensity of the sunlight to achieve different moods and effects in your music video.

3.3. Experiment with Different Camera Angles

Do not be afraid to get creative with your camera angles. A variety of camera angles can add visual interest and make your music video more engaging. Try shooting from different perspectives like low angles, high angles, or even from the ground. Experimenting with camera angles can help you capture unique shots and convey different emotions or story elements. So go ahead and try out different angles to see what works best for your music video!

3.4. Shoot Multiple Takes

Shooting multiple takes is crucial when you have a limited budget. It allows you to have more options during the editing process and ensures that you have enough usable footage. Do not settle for just one take, even if you think it turned out perfectly. Shoot multiple takes from different angles and perspectives to give yourself more choices later. This way, you can select the best shots and create a more polished and professional-looking music video.

3.5. Capture B-Roll Footage

In addition to the main shots of your music video, make sure to capture plenty of B-roll footage. B-roll footage refers to supplementary footage that can be used to enhance your video during the editing process. This can include close-ups of instruments, interesting backgrounds, or even behind-the-scenes moments. B-roll footage adds visual variety and can help make your music video more dynamic and engaging. So, remember to keep your camera rolling even when you are not filming the main scenes!

4. Editing and Finalizing the Video

Once you have finished filming all the necessary footage, it is time to start editing and finalizing your music video. This is where you bring all the pieces together and create a cohesive visual story. Editing is the process of selecting and arranging the footage to create a seamless narrative. This is also the stage where you can enhance your video by adding effects and transitions. Once you are satisfied with the final edit, it is time to export and share your finished music video with the world.

4.1. Choose an Editing Software

Choosing the right editing software is crucial for creating a no-budget music video. There are several free or low-cost options available such as iMovie, Windows Movie Maker, or Shortcut. Consider your computer's operating system and the features you require. Look for software that allows you to easily import and edit your footage, add effects and transitions, and export the final video in a high-quality format. Take some time to explore different editing software options and choose the one that best suits your needs and familiarity.

4.2. Import and Organize Footage

Once you have chosen your editing software, the next step is to import and organize the footage you have filmed. Connect your camera or device to your computer and transfer the video files. Create a new project in your chosen editing software and import the footage into the media library. Organize your clips into folders or bins based on scenes or categories to ensure easy access and smooth workflow. This will help you locate the specific shots you need when it comes to editing the video.

4.3. Edit the Video

Editing the video is where the magic happens. Start by arranging your clips in the desired order to create a cohesive storyline. Trim or cut out any unnecessary footage and rearrange scenes to enhance the visual flow. Experiment with different cuts, pacing, and transitions to create the desired impact. Ensure a balance between visuals and the synchronization with the music. Remember to respect the rhythm and beats of the song. Do not be afraid to make creative decisions as you weave the footage together to bring your music video to life.

4.4. Add Effects and Transitions

Adding effects and transitions can elevate the overall look and feel of your music video. Consider the mood and style of your video and choose the effects accordingly. Common effects include color grading, motion effects, and filters. Transitions help smooth the cuts between different scenes, and you can use several types like fades, dissolves, or slides. Be careful not to overdo it, as too many effects can distract from the main content. Aim for a seamless and visually appealing integration of effects and transitions to enhance the viewing experience.

4.5. Export and Share the Final Video

Once you are satisfied with the final edit, it is time to export and share your music video. In your editing software, choose the appropriate settings for exporting, such as resolution, format, and compression. It is recommended to export in a high-quality format to ensure the best viewing experience. After exporting, double-check the video file to ensure it plays smoothly without any glitches or issues. Finally, it is time to share your music video with the world. Upload it to video sharing platforms like YouTube, Vimeo, or social media platforms to showcase your creative work to a wider audience.

Chapter34

Make Money on YouTube

YOUTUBE HAS PROVIDED users with an extraordinary platform to earn money. YouTubers, both young and old, are making millions of dollars through exceptional video content. For example, 8-year-old Evan rakes in $1 million a year through his channel, EvanTubeHD.

IT IS OBVIOUS THAT YouTube offers exciting opportunities to make money online. However, generating a revenue in millions requires exceptional talent, efforts, and a little bit of luck.

Below are 4 ways you can make money on YouTube.

1. Become a YouTube Partner

Join the YouTube Partner Program to earn money through advertisements and paid subscriptions. The program enables you to partner with YouTube and split the money you generate via ads. Thus, the YouTube Partner Program offers an amazingly simple and convenient way to make money.

USEFUL TIPS:

• Enable your account for monetization. To do this go to the monetization tab in your account's settings. Then, click **Enable My Account**. This option will appear only if your account is in good standing and has not been disabled for monetization. Finally, follow the on-screen steps to accept the YouTube monetization agreement.

- Ensure your video meets YouTube's video[1] monetization criteria. [2]Violation of any one of these guidelines can make your video ineligible for monetization.

- Integrate your YouTube and AdSense accounts to receive revenue.

2. Incorporate paid product placements

YouTube allows users to have paid product placements in their videos. Therefore, you can get paid to integrate a third-party's brand, products, and services with your content.

USEFUL TIPS

- SEVERAL BRANDS LIKE to have their products placed in quality videos. However, partner only with brands whose products align with your video content.

- In-your-face advertising can leave viewers with a jarring video experience. Therefore, present your products in a natural and seamless fashion.

- Product placements are a tedious process and take time to materialize. Therefore, approach brands as early as possible to begin working on your video.

For example, look at the below video. YouTuber Rosanna Pansino mentions the products she uses to make cookie pops. The product has been tied into the video in a subtle manner.

---

1. https://support.google.com/youtube/answer/97527

2. https://support.google.com/youtube/answer/97527

NOTE: Product placements will have to comply with YouTube's ad policies[3].

---

3. https://support.google.com/youtube/answer/188570?topic=30084&ctx=topic&hl=en-GB

3. Reach out to sponsors

THERE ARE SEVERAL ADVANTAGES to signing up sponsors. Firstly, sponsorships are effective in making money on videos that have already been shot. Secondly, YouTube creators do not have to identify prospective sponsors before producing the video. Lastly, YouTubers can sign up sponsors themselves to eliminate go-betweens and generate more revenue.

USEFUL TIPS:

• BUILD A LARGE AUDIENCE and upload intriguing videos to attract sponsors.

• Draft a good sponsorship proposal. Include a brief description of your channel, target demographics, average monthly views, and number of subscribers.

• Target sponsors whose products and services align with your content.

• Reach out to sponsors through social network, referrals, and official websites for sponsorship requests.

4. Promote your products on YouTube

People often overlook the potential of indirect monetization methods. One of the most effective ways to make money is to promote your products and services via YouTube. Therefore, focus on selling free and engaging content to prospective customers.

USEFUL TIPS:

• Create engaging content around your merchandise to compel viewers to make a purchase. For instance, if you are a fashion designer, produce a video to showcase your designs. You can include annotations to highlight the price of the products. In addition, you can also create "how to use this product" tutorials.

• Add links to purchase your product in the video description.

In conclusion, familiarize yourself with the assorted options available to earn money on YouTube. Follow the above strategy too rich and famous.

Interested in getting your YouTube video discovered by masses of targeted fans? Click this link: www.promolta.com[4]

---

4.   http://www.promolta.com/

Chapter 35

Tips for Creating Effective Marketing Videos

1. Getting Started

To create effective marketing videos, it is important to start with a clear plan. This involves determining your target audience, defining your video's purpose, and planning its content. By taking the time to carefully consider these factors, you can ensure that your video will resonate with your intended viewers and effectively convey your message. Additionally, it is crucial to remember that video is a powerful medium that can captivate and engage viewers, so it is worth investing the effort to create a high-quality video that reflects positively on your business.

1.1. Determine your target audience.

Before diving into creating your marketing video, it is essential to determine your target audience. By understanding who your video is aimed at, you can tailor your content to meet their needs and preferences. Consider factors such as demographics, interests, and purchasing behaviors of your ideal viewers. Conducting market research or analyzing data about your current customer base can provide valuable insights that will help you create a video that effectively speaks to your target audience and increases the likelihood of engaging and converting them.

1.2. Define your video's purpose.

Defining the purpose of your marketing video is crucial to ensure its effectiveness. Ask yourself what you want to achieve with the video. Are you aiming to increase brand awareness, generate leads, promote a specific product or service, educate your audience, or something else? Clearly outlining your video's purpose will guide its development and allow you to create content that is aligned with your goals. By having a well-defined purpose, you can ensure that your video delivers a clear and focused message to your viewers.

1.3. Plan your video's content.

Planning the content of your marketing video involves determining the key messages you want to convey, organizing your ideas, and creating a storyboard. Start by identifying the main points or information you want to get across to your audience. Then, arrange these points in a logical order that tells a story or guides viewers through a specific journey. A well-structured video keeps viewers engaged and makes it easier for them to grasp and remember the information you are presenting. Additionally, creating a storyboard will help you visualize the shots, transitions, and overall flow of your video, making the production process smoother.

2. Filming Techniques

When it comes to creating effective marketing videos, understanding the right filming techniques is crucial. These techniques can help enhance the overall quality and impact of your video. To start with, using good lighting is essential. Proper lighting not only improves visibility but also sets the mood and creates a professional look. Additionally, framing your shots effectively is important to ensure that the subject is well-centered and visually appealing. Another key aspect is capturing clear audio. Poor audio quality can distract viewers and detract from the message you are trying to convey. Lastly, do not be afraid to utilize different camera angles to add variety and visual interest to your video. Experiment with different perspectives to showcase your product or service in the most viable way.

2.1. Use good lighting.

Using good lighting is crucial when filming marketing videos. Proper lighting can make a significant difference in the overall quality and impact of your video. Ensure that the subject is well-lit and evenly illuminated, avoiding harsh shadows or overexposure. Natural light can work wonders, so consider shooting near a window or outdoors. If shooting indoors, invest in affordable lighting equipment or use household lamps strategically to create a well-lit environment. By using good lighting, you will enhance the visual appeal of your video and make it more engaging for your audience.

2.2. Frame your shots effectively.

When it comes to creating effective marketing videos, framing your shots effectively is key. Pay attention to composition and ensure that your subject is well-centered within the frame. Use the rule of thirds to create a visually pleasing and balanced shot. Experiment with different angles and perspectives to add depth and interest to your video. Keep in mind the purpose of each shot and how it contributes to the overall story or message. By framing your shots effectively, you will create a visually appealing video that captures your audience's attention.

2.3. Capture clear audio.

Clear audio is essential for creating effective marketing videos. Poor audio quality can detract from the overall impact of your video, even if the visuals are stunning. Invest in a good microphone to capture high-quality sound. Consider using a lapel or shotgun microphone for interviews or voiceovers. Pay attention to background noise and try to eliminate or minimize it during filming. If needed, record audio separately and synchronize it with your footage during the editing process. By capturing clear audio, you will ensure that your message is conveyed effectively and that your viewers can fully engage with your video.

2.4. Utilize different camera angles.

To create visually captivating marketing videos, do not be afraid to utilize different camera angles. By incorporating various camera angles, you can add depth, perspective, and excitement to your video. Experiment with wide shots, close-ups, and even aerial shots if possible. Different angles can highlight specific details, emphasize emotions, or provide a unique viewpoint. Remember to consider the context and purpose of each shot when deciding on camera angles. By incorporating a range of camera angles, you will keep your audience engaged and provide them with a dynamic viewing experience.

3. Editing and Production

Once you have filmed your footage, it is time to dive into the editing and production process. This stage is crucial in creating a visually appealing and engaging marketing video. By skillfully editing your footage and adding the right elements, you can make your video stand out from the crowd and effectively convey your message to your target audience.

3.1. Choose the right video editing software.

Choosing the right video editing software is essential to achieve professional-looking results. There are many options available, ranging from beginner-friendly to advanced platforms. Consider your editing needs, budget, and skill level when selecting software. Popular choices include Adobe Premiere Pro, Final Cut Pro, and iMovie. Take the time to explore different options and find the software that best suits your requirements.

3.2. Trim and arrange your footage.

Trimming and arranging your footage is a crucial step in the editing process. Start by reviewing your footage and identifying the best clips that align with your video's purpose and message. Trim any unnecessary or repetitive parts to keep the video concise and engaging. Arrange your clips in a logical sequence that flows smoothly. By organizing your footage effectively, you can create a cohesive and engaging narrative for your marketing video.

3.3. Add captions or subtitles.

Adding captions or subtitles to your marketing video can enhance its accessibility and reach. Not only do captions make your video more inclusive for viewers with hearing impairments, but they also cater to those who prefer to watch videos without sound or are in a noisy environment. Additionally, captions or subtitles can help reinforce important points or highlight key information. Ensure that the text is clear, easy to read, and synchronized accurately with the audio.

3.4. Incorporate relevant music or sound effects.

Music and sound effects are powerful tools that can evoke emotions and enhance the overall impact of your marketing video. Choose background music that aligns with the tone and message of your video. Consider using royalty-free music or licensed tracks to avoid copyright issues. Additionally, incorporating relevant sound effects can add depth and realism to your visuals. Experiment with different options and find the right balance between music, dialogue, and sound effects to create a captivating audio experience for your viewers.

3.5. Include your branding elements.

Including your branding elements in your marketing video is essential for reinforcing your brand identity and making an impression on your audience. Incorporate your logo, color scheme, and typography in strategic places throughout the video. Consistency is key, so ensure that your branding elements align with your overall marketing strategy. By including these visual cues, you can strengthen brand recognition and create a cohesive visual experience for your viewers.

4. Promoting Your Video

Once you have created your marketing video, it is time to promote it to reach a wider audience. There are several effective strategies you can employ to maximize the visibility of your video. First, upload your video to popular platforms such as YouTube and Vimeo, as these platforms have a large user base. This will increase the chances of your video being discovered by potential viewers. Next, optimize your video's title and description by using keywords that are relevant to your target audience. This will help your video appear in search results when users are looking for content related to your industry or topic. Additionally, do not forget to share your video on social media platforms like Facebook, Twitter, and Instagram. These platforms allow you to reach your existing followers and expand your reach through shares and retweets. Lastly, engaging with your audience through comments and responses is crucial. Respond to comments, answer questions, and encourage discussion to foster a sense of community around your video.

4.1. Upload your video to popular platforms.

When it comes to promoting your marketing video, uploading it to popular platforms is essential. Platforms like YouTube and Vimeo have a massive user base and offer great visibility for your video. By uploading your video to these platforms, you increase the likelihood of it being discovered by a wider audience. Moreover, these platforms provide tools for analytics and metrics, allowing you to track the performance of your video and make informed decisions about your marketing strategy. So, make sure to create accounts on these platforms if you have not already and start sharing your video with the world!

4.2. Optimize your video's title and description.

Optimizing your video's title and description is vital for better visibility and search engine optimization. To do this, choose a title that accurately represents the content of your video and includes relevant keywords that your target audience might use when searching. In the description, provide a summary of what viewers can expect from your video and include links to your website or other related resources. This will not only help viewers understand the context of your video but also drive traffic to your website. Remember to keep the title concise and engaging and provide a captivating description to entice viewers to click and watch your video.

4.3. Share your video on social media.

Social media platforms are powerful tools for promoting your marketing video. Share your video on platforms like Facebook, Twitter, and Instagram to reach a larger audience and generate more views. When sharing, make sure to create engaging captions and include relevant hashtags to increase discoverability. You can also collaborate with influencers or industry partners who have a substantial following on social media. By sharing your video on their accounts or having them promote it, you can tap into their audience and expand your reach even further. Remember to encourage your followers to share the video as well, as this can lead to viral spread and increased exposure.

4.4. Engage with your audience through comments and responses Engaging with your audience is crucial for building a strong connection and fostering a loyal following. When viewers leave comments on your marketing video, take the time to respond to them. Answer any questions they might have, thank them for their feedback, and encourage further discussion. This not only shows that you value their opinions and appreciate their engagement but also helps to build a sense of community around your video. People are more likely to share and recommend your video if they feel a personal connection with you. So, be active in the comment section, show genuine interest in your viewers, and create an engaging dialogue to keep them coming back for more.

Chapter 36

Tips for Optimizing Your Music Website for Search Engines

1. Importance of Search Engine Optimization (SEO)

Search Engine Optimization (SEO) plays a crucial role in the success of your music website. By optimizing your site, you can improve its visibility in search engine results and attract more visitors. With most people using search engines to discover contemporary music and artists, it is essential to ensure that your website appears prominently in relevant search queries. By implementing effective SEO strategies, you can increase your website's chances of ranking higher, resulting in more organic traffic and potential fans.

1.1. Increase visibility and attract more visitors.

Implementing proper SEO techniques on your music website can significantly increase its visibility and attract more visitors. By optimizing your website's content, meta tags, and descriptions, you can improve its search engine ranking and make it more appealing to potential fans searching for relevant keywords. Higher visibility means more exposure to your music, which can lead to an increase in visitor traffic. So, do not overlook the importance of SEO in driving more visitors to your music website and potentially expanding your fan base.

1.2. Drive organic traffic to your music website.

When it comes to driving organic traffic to your music website, SEO is a powerful tool. By utilizing effective keyword research and implementation strategies, you can optimize your website for specific search terms related to your music niche. This increases the chances of your website appearing prominently in search engine results, driving targeted organic traffic to your site. With a well-optimized website, you can attract relevant visitors who are more likely to engage with your music and become fans. So, by focusing on SEO, you can drive organic traffic and potentially grow your fan base in a sustainable and effective way.

2. Keyword Research and Implementation

Implementing effective keywords is crucial for optimizing your music website for search engines. By conducting thorough keyword research, you can identify relevant terms that resonate with your music niche and target audience. This will help you understand what potential visitors are searching for and enable you to optimize

your content accordingly. Utilizing industry-specific keywords in your website content, including blog posts, music descriptions, and artist biographies, will optimize your website's visibility and increase organic traffic. Additionally, adopting long-tail keywords, which are longer and more specific phrases, can provide better ranking opportunities as they align with users' specific queries. By incorporating keywords strategically throughout your website, you can enhance your search engine optimization efforts and attract more visitors.

2.1. Identify relevant keywords for your music niche.

Identifying relevant keywords for your music niche is a crucial step in optimizing your music website. To begin, consider the specific genre, style, or theme of your music and brainstorm associated keywords. You can also explore tools like Google Keyword Planner, SEMrush, or Moz Keyword Explorer to discover popular search terms related to your niche. Additionally, analyzing competitor websites can provide insights into the keywords they are targeting. By understanding the language and terminology commonly used in your music niche, you can effectively optimize your website with relevant keywords that align with users' search queries. This will increase the visibility of your music website and attract more targeted traffic.

2.2. Optimize website content with targeted keywords.

Optimizing your website content with targeted keywords is essential for improving search engine visibility and driving organic traffic. Once you have identified relevant keywords for your music niche, strategically incorporate them throughout your website. These keywords should be seamlessly integrated into your page titles, headers, body text, image alt attributes, and meta tags. However, it is crucial to find a balance and avoid keyword stuffing, which can negatively impact your website's ranking. Write compelling, unique content that aligns with user intent and optimizes it with the identified keywords. By doing so, search engines will recognize the relevance of your content and display your website higher in the search results, increasing its visibility to potential visitors.

2.3. Utilize long-tail keywords for better ranking opportunities.

To improve your website's ranking opportunities, it is beneficial to utilize long-tail keywords. These keywords are longer and more specific phrases that target a narrower audience. For example, instead of targeting a broad keyword like "pop music," you can focus on a long-tail keyword like "upbeat pop dance songs." Since long-tail keywords have lower competition, they provide better chances of ranking higher in search engine results. Incorporating long-tail keywords throughout your website, such as in blog articles or product descriptions, can attract visitors who are specifically searching for what you offer. By understanding the intent behind users' search queries and tailoring your content to meet their needs, you can optimize your music website for better search engine rankings and increase your chances of attracting relevant traffic.

3. On-Page Optimization Techniques

On-page optimization techniques play a crucial role in improving the visibility and search engine ranking of your music website. By implementing these techniques, you can enhance the overall user experience and increase the chances of your website being discovered by potential visitors. These techniques include optimizing meta tags and descriptions, creating unique and engaging page titles, enhancing website speed and mobile responsiveness, and improving user experience with intuitive navigation. Each of these aspects contributes to making your website more search engine-friendly and user-friendly, thereby boosting its chances of appearing higher in search engine results.

3.1. Optimize meta tags and descriptions.

Optimizing meta tags and descriptions is an important aspect of on-page optimization for your music website. Meta tags provide search engines with information about your web pages, while descriptions offer a summary of the page content. By including relevant keywords in your meta tags and descriptions, you can make it easier for search engines to understand the context and relevance of your website. This increases the likelihood of your website appearing in relevant search results and attracting more organic traffic. Additionally, well-optimized meta tags and descriptions can also improve the click-through rate of your website, as they provide users with a clear idea of what they can expect from your web pages.

3.2. Create unique and engaging page titles.

Creating unique and engaging page titles is a key on-page optimization technique for your music website. Page titles appear as the clickable headline in search engine results and act as a concise summary of the page content. By crafting compelling and descriptive page titles, you can grab the attention of users and entice them to click on your website. Including relevant keywords in your page titles can also improve your website's visibility in search engine rankings. It is important to ensure that each page on your website has a unique title that accurately represents the content it offers. This not only helps search engines understand the relevance of your pages but also makes it easier for users to navigate your website.

3.3. Enhance website speed and mobile responsiveness.

Enhancing the speed and mobile responsiveness of your music website is crucial for both search engine optimization and user experience. Slow-loading websites can result in higher bounce rates and lower search engine rankings. By optimizing your website's speed, you can improve the overall user experience and keep visitors engaged. Additionally, with an increasing number of people accessing the internet through mobile devices, it is essential to ensure that your website is mobile-friendly and responsive across different screen sizes. This not only caters to a larger audience but also improves your website's chances of ranking higher in mobile search results. Optimizing website speed and mobile responsiveness can significantly impact the visibility and success of your music website.

3.4. Improve user experience with intuitive navigation.

A seamless and intuitive navigation system is vital to improve the user experience on your music website. Easy navigation helps visitors find the desired content quickly and enhances their overall satisfaction with your website. This, in turn, can lead to longer visit durations and increased engagement, positively impacting your search engine rankings. Implementing a clear and organized navigation menu, using descriptive labels for categories and pages, and providing search functionality can improve the user experience. Remember to prioritize simplicity and user-friendliness as complex navigation systems can confuse and frustrate visitors. By focusing on intuitive navigation, you can make it easier for both users and search engines to explore and navigate your music website effectively.

4. Building High-Quality Backlinks

Building high-quality backlinks is crucial for improving the visibility and ranking of your music website in search engines.

Backlinks are links from other websites that point to your site, indicating its relevance and credibility. To build high-quality backlinks, you can seek opportunities for guest blogging and collaborations. This involves reaching out to other music-related websites or blogs and offering to write guest posts or collaborate on content. By doing so, you can not only gain exposure to a wider audience but also include links back to your website, boosting its authority and search engine rankings. It is important to ensure that the websites you collaborate with are reputable and relevant to your music niche for the best results.

4.1. Seek opportunities for guest blogging and collaborations.

Seeking opportunities for guest blogging and collaborations is a wonderful way to build high-quality backlinks for your music website. Guest blogging involves authoring articles or blog posts for other music-related websites or blogs in exchange for including a link back to your own site. This not only helps drive traffic to your website but also improves its search engine visibility and credibility. Look for websites that are popular in your music niche and reach out to them with your proposal. Collaborating with other musicians or music influencers is another effective strategy. You can create joint content, such as videos, podcasts, or interviews, and promote them through your respective websites and social media channels. This way, you can attract more visitors and build valuable backlinks at the same time.

4.2. Engage with music communities and forums.

Engaging with music communities and forums is a smart move to build high-quality backlinks for your music website. Join online communities, forums, and discussion boards that cater to music enthusiasts and actively participate by sharing your expertise, insights, and valuable advice. Include your website link in your forum signature or when relevant to the discussion. By providing helpful and relevant contributions to the community, you can establish your credibility and attract attention from other members, who may then visit your website and potentially link back to it. It is important to remember that self-promotion should be done subtly and in a non-spammy manner to ensure a positive reputation within the community.

4.3. Utilize social media platforms for link building.

Social media platforms offer great opportunities for link building and boosting the visibility of your music website. You can share your website content on platforms like Facebook, Twitter, Instagram, and YouTube, including links to relevant pages or blog posts. Engage with your audience by posting engaging content, replying to comments, and participating in discussions. By building a strong social media presence and regularly sharing valuable content, you can attract more followers and increase the likelihood of others sharing your links. Additionally, you can actively seek collaborations with other musicians or music-related accounts on social media. This can involve featuring each other's content, mentioning one another in posts, or cross promoting your websites. Such collaborations can help expand your reach and generate high-quality backlinks from reputable sources.

Chapter 37

Get More Visits to Your Website

1. Increase Your Website's Visibility

Increasing your website's visibility is crucial to attract more visitors. By implementing the right strategies, you can improve your search engine rankings and gain more traffic. One way to achieve this is by optimizing your website for search engines. This involves using relevant keywords, meta tags, and creating high-quality content. Additionally, using social media platforms can promote your website. Make sure to share your content, interact with your audience, and engage in conversations to expand your reach. Another effective method is collaborating with influencers. By partnering with influencers in your industry, you can tap into their follower base and capture the attention of a wider audience.

1.1. Optimize your website for search engines.

Optimizing your website for search engines is essential to improve its visibility and attract more visitors. Focus on using relevant keywords throughout your website, including in the page titles, headers, and content. Conduct keyword research to identify the terms your target audience is searching for and incorporate them naturally into your website. Additionally, create informative meta tags that accurately describe your webpages. High-quality content is also crucial, as search engines prioritize websites that provide valuable and engaging information. Regularly update your content and ensure it is well-structured and easy to read. By implementing these optimization techniques, you can enhance your website's ranking on search engine results pages.

1.2. Use social media to promote your website.

Social media platforms offer excellent opportunities to promote your website and attract more visitors. Create profiles on popular platforms like Facebook, Instagram, Twitter, and LinkedIn, and regularly share relevant content from your website. Interact with your audience by responding to comments, messages, and mentions. Engage in conversations and provide valuable insights or advice. Utilize relevant hashtags and join industry-related groups or communities to expand your reach. Consider running paid advertising campaigns on social media platforms to target specific demographics and increase your website's visibility. By strategically using social media, you can effectively promote your website and drive more traffic.

1.3. Collaborate with influencers to reach a wider audience
Collaborating with influencers is a powerful way to reach a wider audience and increase your website's visibility. Identify influencers in your industry who align with your brand values and have a substantial following. Reach out to them with a personalized message explaining why you believe a collaboration would be mutually beneficial. This could include hosting joint webinars, guest blogging on each other's websites, or creating collaborative content. When influencers share your content or recommend your website, their followers are more likely to visit and engage with your site. This helps you expand your reach and gain credibility within your target market. Building relationships with influencers can significantly boost your website's visibility and attract new visitors.

2. Create Engaging Content
Creating engaging content is crucial for attracting visitors to your website. By providing valuable and interesting information, you can capture the attention of your target audience and encourage them to explore your site further. There are many ways to create engaging content, such as writing compelling blog posts, producing informative videos or podcasts, offering free resources or downloads, and encouraging user-generated content through contests or giveaways. By implementing these strategies, you can provide value to your visitors and keep them coming back for more.

2.1. Write compelling blog posts.
Writing compelling blog posts is an effective way to engage your website visitors. By sharing informative and well-written content, you can establish yourself as an authority in your industry and attract a loyal audience. Make sure to choose topics that are relevant to your target audience's interests and provide valuable insights or solutions to their problems. Use a conversational and friendly tone to connect with your readers and keep them engaged throughout the article. Additionally, incorporating relevant keywords can help optimize

your blog posts for search engines, increasing the visibility of your website.

2.2. Produce informative videos or podcasts.

Producing informative videos or podcasts can be a highly engaging way to connect with your audience. Visual and auditory content has the power to captivate viewers and listeners, allowing you to deliver your message in a more engaging and memorable way. Choose topics that are of interest to your target audience and provide valuable information or entertainment. Ensure that your videos or podcasts are well-produced and have high-quality audio and video to enhance the user experience. By incorporating these multimedia elements into your content strategy, you can increase the likelihood of attracting and retaining visitors to your website.

2.3. Offer free resources or downloads to attract visitors.

Offering free resources or downloads is a wonderful way to attract visitors to your website. These can include e-books, templates, guides, or any other valuable content that your target audience might find useful. By providing these resources for free, you not only demonstrate your expertise and willingness to help but also give visitors a reason to return to your site. Promote these resources through your website, social media channels, and email newsletters to reach a wider audience. By offering something of value without asking for anything in return, you can build trust and credibility with your visitors, increasing the chances of them becoming regular readers or customers.

2.4. Encouraging user-generated content through contests or giveaways

Encouraging user-generated content through contests or giveaways is an effective way to engage your website visitors and foster a sense of community. By running contests or giveaways, you incentivize your audience to actively participate and contribute to your website. This can include submitting photos, videos, testimonials, or any other form of user-generated content related to your brand or industry. Not only does this create valuable content for your website, but it also encourages visitors to share and promote your brand on their own social media platforms, thereby increasing your website's visibility. By nurturing this interactive and collaborative environment, you can strengthen the relationship with your audience and attract more visitors to your website.

3. Utilize Online Advertising

Online advertising is an effective way to get more visits to your website. By using targeted ads on search engines, displaying ads on relevant websites or social media platforms, and retargeting visitors with personalized ads, you can increase your website's visibility and conversions. Online ads allow you to reach a wider audience who are actively searching for products or services like yours. They provide an opportunity to showcase your offerings to potential customers, attract their attention, and drive them to your website. By utilizing online advertising strategies, you can effectively promote your website and attract more visitors.

3.1. Run targeted ads on search engines.

To increase your website's visibility and drive more visits, running targeted ads on search engines is a smart move. Search ads allow you to appear at the top of search engine result pages when users search for keywords related to our business. By targeting specific keywords and demographics, you can reach a highly relevant audience who are actively looking for products or services like yours. These ads provide a direct link to your website, making it easy for users to visit and explore what you have to offer. With strategic ad placements and compelling ad copy, you can attract qualified traffic to your website and increase your chances of conversions.

3.2. Display ads on relevant websites or social media platforms. Another effective way to increase your website's visits is by displaying ads on relevant websites or social media platforms. These platforms offer targeted advertising options that allow you to reach your desired audience based on their interests, demographics, and online behavior. By placing ads on websites or social media platforms that are frequented by your target audience, you can expose your brand to a larger user base and drive more traffic to your website. These display ads can be highly visual with compelling images or videos to catch the attention of users and entice them to click through to your website.

3.3. Retarget visitors with personalized ads to increase conversions Retargeting visitors with personalized ads is a powerful technique to increase conversions on your website. When visitors leave your website without taking any action, you can continue to engage with them through targeted ads as they browse other websites or social media platforms. By using cookies and tracking pixels, you can identify those visitors and deliver personalized ads that remind them of your offerings and bring them back to your website. These ads can offer exclusive discounts, promotions, or product recommendations to entice visitors to make a purchase or complete a desired action. By staying top-of-mind and providing tailored messaging, you can effectively increase conversions and drive more visits to your website.

4. Improve Website Performance and User Experience Improving website performance and user experience is crucial for attracting more visitors to your website. Users expect websites to load quickly and provide a seamless browsing experience. By optimizing website speed and loading times, ensuring mobile responsiveness, simplifying navigation, and implementing clear call-to-actions, you can enhance the overall user experience. These improvements will not only increase the chances of visitors staying on your site but also encourage them to take the desired actions, such as making a purchase or filling out a contact form. So, take the necessary steps to improve your website's performance and user experience to drive more traffic and achieve your business goals.

4.1. Optimize website speed and loading times.

One of the key factors in improving website performance is optimizing the speed and loading times. Slow-loading websites can be frustrating for visitors and lead to high bounce rates. To optimize your website's speed, you can compress images and files, minify code, and leverage browser caching. Additionally, using a content delivery network (CDN) can help distribute your website's content across multiple servers, reducing the time it takes for users to access your site. By implementing these strategies, you can ensure that your website loads quickly and efficiently, providing a better user experience and increasing the chances of visitors staying on your site.

4.2. Ensure mobile responsiveness for a seamless browsing experience in today's mobile-driven world, ensuring mobile responsiveness is essential for a seamless browsing experience. With the increasing number of users accessing websites through mobile devices, it is crucial to optimize your website's design and layout to adapt to different screen sizes. Responsive web design allows your website to automatically adjust its layout, content, and functionality to provide the optimal user experience across all devices. By ensuring mobile responsiveness, you not only cater to mobile users but also improve your website's visibility in search engine rankings, as search engines prioritize mobile-friendly websites. So, make sure your website is mobile-responsive to attract more visitors and keep them engaged with your content.

4.3. Simplify navigation and improve website layout.

Improving website navigation and layout is crucial for enhancing user experience and increasing visitor engagement. A cluttered and confusing navigation menu can make it difficult for users to find the information they are looking for, leading to frustration and high bounce rates. Simplify your website's navigation by organizing your menu into logical categories and using clear, descriptive labels. Additionally, focus on improving the overall layout of your website by ensuring a clean and visually appealing design. Use whitespace effectively, prioritize important content, and make sure the layout is consistent across all pages. By simplifying navigation and improving website layout, you can provide a user-friendly experience that encourages visitors to explore more of your website and stay engaged with your content.

4.4. Implement clear call-to-actions to guide visitors towards desired actions.

To guide visitors towards desired actions, it is crucial to implement clear and compelling call-to-actions (CTAs) throughout your website. CTAs prompt visitors to take specific actions, such as making a purchase, signing up for a newsletter, or contacting you for more information. To create effective CTAs, use action-oriented language and make them visually stand out from the rest of your website's content. Place CTAs strategically in prominent locations, such as at the end of blog posts or on product pages. Additionally, ensure that CTAs are easy to understand and provide clear instructions on what visitors need to do next. By implementing clear CTAs, you can guide visitors towards the actions you want them to take, increasing conversions and achieving your website's goals.

Chapter 38

What Your Website Needs to Increase Traffic and Sales
1. Importance of Website Traffic

Website traffic is crucial for the success of any online business. It represents the number of visitors that come to your website and has a direct impact on your sales and revenue. Without sufficient traffic, your website will not be able to generate leads, attract potential customers, or increase conversions. By driving more traffic to your website, you can increase the visibility of your brand, reach a wider audience, and grow your business.

1.1. Attracting the Right Audience

Attracting the right audience to your website is essential for driving targeted traffic that is more likely to convert into customers. Understanding your target audience's demographics, interests, and behaviors can help you create content and marketing strategies that resonate with them. By conducting market research and utilizing audience segmentation, you can tailor your website's content and advertisements to effectively attract the right audience and increase engagement and conversions.

1.2. Increasing Organic Search Traffic

Increasing organic search traffic is a key aspect of driving more visitors to your website. By optimizing your website's content for search engines, you can improve your rankings in search engine results pages and attract organic traffic. This can be achieved through keyword research and optimization, creating high-quality and relevant content, and optimizing meta tags and descriptions.

Implementing search engine optimization (SEO) strategies can help your website appear higher in search results, leading to increased visibility and traffic.

1.3. Utilizing Social Media Platforms

Social media platforms offer a valuable opportunity to increase website traffic and reach a wider audience. By strategically utilizing social media platforms such as Facebook, Instagram, and Twitter, businesses can promote their website content, products, and services to a larger user base. Engaging with followers, sharing informative and entertaining content, and running targeted ad campaigns can drive traffic back to your website. Social media is also a great platform for building brand awareness and establishing a strong online presence.

2. Optimizing Website Design and User Experience

Optimizing website design and user experience is crucial for attracting and retaining visitors. A well-designed website not only improves the overall look and feel but also enhances usability. By implementing user-friendly features and intuitive navigation, users can easily find what they are looking for, leading to a positive experience. Engaging and high-quality content further adds value to the website, keeping visitors engaged and encouraging them to explore more. Additionally, fast loading speed is essential as users often abandon slow-loading websites. By optimizing design, usability, content, and loading speed, websites can create a seamless experience that drives traffic and boosts sales.

2.1. Responsive and Mobile-Friendly Design

Having a responsive and mobile-friendly design is paramount in today's digital landscape. With the increasing use of smartphones and tablets, websites must adapt and provide a seamless experience across different devices. Responsive design ensures that the website automatically adjusts its layout and elements to fit various screen sizes, ensuring easy navigation and readability. By catering to mobile users, businesses can reach a wider audience and increase traffic. Mobile-friendly websites also improve search engine rankings, as search engines prioritize mobile-friendly sites. Therefore, investing in a responsive design is essential for driving traffic and promoting sales.

2.2. Clear and Intuitive Navigation

Clear and intuitive navigation is key to enhancing the user experience and increasing website traffic. Users should be able to easily navigate through different pages, find relevant information, and complete desired actions. Strategic placement of menus, search bars, and prominent call-to-action buttons can help users find what they need quickly. Avoiding clutter and organizing content into logical sections also improves navigation. Intuitive navigation ensures that visitors spend more time on the website, exploring different pages and products/services. By providing a seamless navigation experience, businesses can keep users engaged and encourage them to convert into customers.

2.3. Engaging and High-Quality Content

Engaging and high-quality content is vital for capturing the attention of visitors and driving them to act. Compelling and informative content not only educates users but also builds trust and credibility. By providing valuable content that addresses users' pain points and offers solutions, businesses can position themselves as authorities in their industry. Incorporating visuals, such as images and videos, can further enhance engagement. Additionally, regularly updating the website with fresh and relevant content keeps visitors coming back for more. Quality content also improves search engine visibility, attracting organic traffic and boosting sales.

2.4. Fast Loading Speed

Fast loading speed is crucial for optimizing website performance and user experience. Users expect websites to load quickly, and slow-loading websites can lead to frustration and abandonment. To improve loading speed, businesses can optimize images, minify CSS and JavaScript files, and leverage caching techniques. Additionally, choosing a reliable hosting provider and regularly monitoring website performance are essential. A fast-loading website not only enhances the user experience but also improves search engine rankings. Search engines prioritize fast-loading websites, leading to higher visibility and increased organic traffic. Therefore, focusing on fast loading speed is crucial for attracting and retaining visitors, boosting sales.

3. Implementing Effective SEO Strategies

Implementing effective SEO strategies is crucial for increasing website traffic and sales. SEO, or search engine optimization, involves optimizing your website to rank higher in search engine results pages. By utilizing various strategies, you can improve your website's visibility and attract more organic traffic. Key elements of effective SEO include keyword research and optimization, on-page SEO techniques, and building quality backlinks. By implementing these strategies, you can enhance your website's visibility, drive targeted traffic, and increase your sales.

3.1. Keyword Research and Optimization

Keyword research and optimization are fundamental to successful SEO. It involves identifying the keywords and phrases that your target audience is likely to search for and incorporating them strategically into your website content. By conducting thorough keyword research, you can identify high-ranking keywords with lower competition and optimize your website accordingly. This helps search engines understand the relevance of your content and improves your chances of appearing in relevant search results. Effective keyword optimization can significantly increase your website's visibility and attract more quality traffic.

3.2. On-Page SEO Techniques

On-page SEO techniques focus on optimizing individual web pages to improve their search engine rankings. This includes optimizing meta tags, title tags, headings, URLs, and image alt tags to make them more search engine friendly. Additionally, it involves optimizing the page content with relevant keywords, providing valuable and unique content and improving the overall user experience. By implementing on-page SEO techniques, you can enhance your website's visibility, increase its relevance to search engines, and attract more targeted traffic.

3.3. Building Quality Backlinks

Building quality backlinks is an essential aspect of off-page SEO. Backlinks are links from external websites that point to your website, indicating its credibility and value. Search engines consider backlinks as a vote of confidence for your website, and the more high-quality backlinks you have, the better your chances of ranking higher in search results. Building quality backlinks involves creating valuable content that naturally attracts links, reaching out to relevant websites for link opportunities, and utilizing social media platforms to promote your content. By building quality backlinks, you can improve your website's authority, visibility, and drive more organic traffic and sales.

4. Conversion Rate Optimization

Conversion rate optimization is a crucial aspect of increasing website traffic and sales. It involves making strategic changes to your website to encourage more visitors to take the desired actions, such as making a purchase or filling out a form. By optimizing your conversion rate, you can improve the overall effectiveness of your online marketing efforts. This section will explore various techniques and strategies that can help you optimize your website's conversion rate.

4.1. Compelling Call-to-Actions

A compelling call-to-action (CTA) is an essential element of any successful website. It is a prompt that urges visitors to take specific action, such as signing up for a newsletter, making a purchase, or contacting your business. By creating compelling CTAs, you can effectively guide your website visitors towards the desired conversions. This section will provide tips and examples for creating compelling CTAs that can significantly increase your website's conversion rate.

4.2. Streamlined Checkout Process

A streamlined checkout process is vital for maximizing conversion rates on e-commerce websites. A lengthy and confusing checkout process can lead to cart abandonment and lost sales. By optimizing the checkout process, you can simplify and streamline the steps required for customers to complete their purchase. This section will discuss best practices for creating a user-friendly checkout process that minimizes friction and increases the likelihood of successful conversions.

4.3. USER REVIEWS AND Testimonials

User reviews and testimonials play a significant role in building trust with potential customers and influencing their purchasing decisions. By showcasing positive feedback from satisfied customers, you can establish credibility and promote confidence in your products or services. This section will explore strategies for gathering and displaying user reviews and testimonials effectively, along with the potential impact they can have on your website's conversion rate.

4.4. Personalization and Targeted Marketing

Personalization and targeted marketing are powerful tools for increasing website traffic and conversions. By tailoring your marketing messages and website content to specific audience segments, you can deliver a more relevant and engaging experience to your visitors. This section will delve into the benefits of personalization and targeted marketing, along with practical tips for implementing these strategies to enhance your website's conversion rate.

Chapter 39

YouTube Video Promotion

1. Introduction

YouTube Video Promotion is an essential tool for content creators and businesses looking to increase their visibility and reach on the platform. With billions of users and videos being uploaded every day, it can be challenging to stand out from the crowd. That is where YouTube Video Promotion comes in. By leveraging various strategies and techniques, you can effectively promote your videos and gain more views, subscribers, and engagement. In this guide, we will explore the purpose and benefits of YouTube Video Promotion, as well as strategies, social media promotion, and paid promotion options to help you achieve your video promotion goals.

1.1. Purpose of YouTube Video Promotion

The purpose of YouTube Video Promotion is to increase the visibility and exposure of your videos on the platform. When you create and upload a video, it is not enough to simply wait for viewers to find it organically. YouTube Video Promotion allows you to actively promote your videos to a wider audience, ensuring that they reach the right people who are interested in your content. Whether you are a content creator looking to grow your subscriber base or a business aiming to increase brand awareness, YouTube Video Promotion helps you achieve your goals by driving more views, engagement, and success on the platform.

1.2. Benefits of YouTube Video Promotion

YouTube Video Promotion offers numerous benefits for content creators and businesses alike. Firstly, it helps you reach a larger audience by increasing the visibility of your videos. By promoting your videos to the right target audience, you can attract more views, subscribers, and engagement. Additionally, YouTube Video Promotion enhances your credibility and authority in your niche, as a higher number of views and engagement signals to viewers that your content is valuable and worth watching. Moreover, it allows you to build a loyal community around your channel by reaching viewers who are genuinely interested in your content. Lastly, YouTube Video Promotion opens opportunities for collaboration with influencers and brands, further expanding your reach and potential for success.

2. Strategies for YouTube Video Promotion

When it comes to promoting your YouTube videos, there are several strategies you can employ to increase visibility and engagement. One of the most important strategies are to create engaging content that captivates the audience. Additionally, optimizing video titles and descriptions with relevant keywords can help improve search rankings and attract more viewers. Utilizing tags and keywords in your videos can also help the YouTube algorithm recommend your content to users interested in related topics. Lastly, collaborating with influencers in your industry can help expand your reach and tap into their existing audience. By implementing these strategies, you can effectively promote your YouTube videos and achieve greater success.

2.1. Creating Engaging Content

Creating engaging content is key to capturing the attention and retaining the interest of your YouTube audience. To achieve this, focus on delivering valuable information, entertaining storytelling, or unique perspectives in your videos. Incorporate high-quality visuals, captivating intros, and clear audio to enhance the overall viewing experience. It is important to pay attention to pacing, keeping your videos concise and engaging from start to finish. Additionally, consider including interactive elements such as polls, quizzes, or calls-to-action to encourage viewer participation and boost engagement. By creating content that resonates with your target audience, you will have a better chance of attracting and retaining viewers.

2.2. Optimizing Video Titles and Descriptions

Optimizing video titles and descriptions is crucial for improving discoverability and attracting more viewers to your YouTube videos. It is important to choose descriptive titles that accurately represent the content of your video and include relevant keywords. Avoid using clickbait or misleading titles, as this can result in a negative user experience and lower engagement. Additionally, optimize your video descriptions by providing a concise summary of the video's content and incorporating relevant keywords naturally. You can also include relevant links, timestamps, and subscribe buttons to make it easier for viewers to navigate and engage with your content. By optimizing your video titles and descriptions, you increase the chances of your videos being recommended to the right audience.

2.3. Utilizing Tags and Keywords

Tags and keywords play a crucial role in helping YouTube understand the context and relevance of your videos. When selecting tags, choose ones that accurately represent the main topics and themes of your video. Use both broad and specific tags to increase the chances of your video appearing in searches and related video recommendations. Additionally, include relevant keywords in your video's metadata, including the title, description, and tags. This will help optimize your video for search engine results and increase visibility. It is important to use tags and keywords that are relevant to your content and align with what your target audience is searching for. By utilizing tags and keywords effectively, you can improve your video's discoverability and attract more viewers.

2.4. Collaborating with Influencers

Collaborating with influencers in your industry can be a powerful strategy to promote your YouTube videos. Find influencers who have a similar target audience and whose content aligns with your brand or niche. Reach out to them with a personalized pitch, showcasing why collaborating would be beneficial for both parties. You can propose collaborations such as featuring each other in videos, creating joint content, or sponsoring their videos. By leveraging the influence and credibility of these influencers, you can tap into their existing audience and gain valuable exposure. This collaboration can help drive more views, increase engagement, and attract new subscribers to your YouTube channel. It is important to choose influencers who genuinely resonate with your brand to ensure the collaboration feels authentic and mutually beneficial.

3. Promoting YouTube Videos on Social Media

Promoting YouTube videos on social media is an essential strategy to increase their visibility and reach a wider audience. By leveraging the power of social media platforms, creators can share their videos and engage with their followers in a more interactive way. Social media allows for easy and quick sharing of YouTube videos with friends, family, and followers. It provides a platform for creators to build a community around their content and encourage discussions and engagement. By actively promoting videos on social media, creators can drive more views, likes, comments, and shares, increasing their video's overall reach and impact.

3.1. Sharing Videos on Facebook

Sharing YouTube videos on Facebook is a wonderful way to promote them to a large and diverse audience. By posting videos on Facebook, creators can take advantage of its massive user base and the platform's features, such as video embedding, autoplay, and tagging. This allows videos to be easily discovered and shared by Facebook users. Additionally, creators can utilize Facebook groups and pages related to their niche or target audience to share their videos with a more specific and engaged community. By actively sharing and promoting videos on Facebook, creators can increase their video's visibility, gain more views, and potentially attract new subscribers to their YouTube channel.

3.2. Tweeting Videos on Twitter

Tweeting YouTube videos on Twitter is an effective way to reach a wide audience and create buzz around the content. With Twitter's fast-paced and real-time nature, creators can share videos and engage with their followers in short, concise messages. Twitter also allows for the use of hashtags and mentions, making it easier to target specific communities or individuals who might be interested in the video. By sharing videos on Twitter, creators can tap into trending topics and conversations, increasing the chances of their videos getting noticed and shared by a wider audience. Additionally, retweets and likes can further amplify the video's reach and potential impact.

3.3. Utilizing Instagram for Video Promotion

Utilizing Instagram for video promotion provides creators with a visually appealing platform to showcase their content. Using visually striking images, captions, and hashtags, creators can capture the attention of Instagram users and entice them to watch their YouTube videos. Instagram Stories and IGTV also offer additional avenues for creators to share their videos with their followers. By utilizing features like swipe up links and engaging captions, creators can direct their Instagram followers to their YouTube channel or specific video, increasing their video's views and engagement. Leveraging the power of Instagram influencers and collaborations can further boost the reach and promotion of YouTube videos on the platform.

3.4. Leveraging LinkedIn for Video Promotion

Leveraging LinkedIn for video promotion might be less conventional, but it can still be an effective strategy for certain types of content. LinkedIn provides a professional and business-oriented platform, making it suitable for videos related to industry insights, tutorials, or thought leadership content. By posting videos on LinkedIn, creators can tap into their professional networks and showcase their expertise and knowledge in their respective fields. LinkedIn groups can also serve as a valuable source of relevant audiences who might be interested in the video's topic. For creators targeting a business or professional audience, leveraging LinkedIn can be a wonderful way to increase their video's visibility and credibility.

4. Paid Promotion Options for YouTube Videos

Paid promotion options provide a way to boost the visibility and reach of your YouTube videos. These options allow you to invest in targeted advertising to reach a wider audience. By utilizing paid promotion, you can increase the chances of your videos being discovered by viewers who may not have come across them

organically. Paid promotion options include YouTube Ads, sponsored content on other channels, and influencer marketing campaigns.

4.1. YouTube Ads

YouTube Ads are a popular method of promoting YouTube videos. These ads appear before, during, or after other YouTube videos, reaching a large number of viewers. With YouTube Ads, you can choose between different ad formats such as skippable or non-skippable ads, bumper ads, display ads, overlay ads, and sponsored cards. Ad targeting options allow you to reach specific demographics, interests, and locations, ensuring your videos are seen by the right audience. By investing in YouTube Ads, you can effectively increase the visibility and engagement of your videos.

4.2. Sponsored Content on Other Channels

Another paid promotion option for YouTube videos is sponsored content on other channels. This involves collaborating with popular YouTube channels or content creators to feature your videos or promote your channel to their audience. By leveraging the established audience of these channels, you can tap into new viewers who may have similar interests. Sponsored content can take the form of video integrations, shoutouts, or dedicated video reviews. This method allows for increased exposure and credibility, as viewers are more likely to trust recommendations from channels they already follow.

4.3. Influencer Marketing Campaigns

Influencer marketing campaigns are another effective way to promote YouTube videos. Influencers are individuals with a large following and influence on social media platforms. By partnering with influencers relevant to your niche or target audience, you can leverage their reach and credibility to promote your videos. This can be done through sponsored content, where the influencer incorporates your video into their content, or through dedicated reviews and endorsements. The key is to find influencers whose audience aligns with your target audience, ensuring your videos are seen by the right viewers and increasing the chances of engagement and subscriptions.

Chapter 40

Event Promotional Strategies

1. Social media promotion

When it comes to promoting your event, social media platforms are powerful tools to reach a wide audience. Utilizing Facebook is a wonderful way to create an event page where you can provide all the necessary information, engage with potential attendees through comments, and even run targeted ads to reach specific demographics. Engaging with Twitter allows you to tweet about your event, use relevant hashtags to increase visibility, and interact with users who express interest or ask questions. Leveraging Instagram enables you to share visually appealing content, such as photos and videos, which showcase the excitement and highlights of your event, while using popular event-related hashtags to attract attention and generate buzz.

1.1. Utilizing Facebook

Facebook offers various features to effectively promote your event. By creating an event page, you can provide vital details like the date, location, and ticket information. It is essential to regularly update the page by posting engaging content, such as sneak peeks, behind-the-scenes photos, and promotional videos. Encourage attendees to share the event with their friends and networks, increasing the visibility organically. Additionally, utilizing Facebook's targeted advertising options allows you to create custom ads to reach specific demographics and interests, ensuring your event reaches the right audience.

1.2. Engaging with Twitter

Twitter offers a dynamic platform to engage with potential attendees and create buzz for your event. Start by creating a hashtag specifically for your event, making it easier for users to find related content and conversations. Utilize this hashtag in your tweets to increase visibility and encourage others to join the conversation. Engaging with users who express interest or ask questions about your event is crucial. Respond promptly and provide helpful information to build a positive reputation and encourage attendance. Tweeting updates, exciting announcements, and live coverage during the event will keep followers engaged and foster a sense of excitement and anticipation.

1.3. Leveraging Instagram

Instagram, a visually driven platform, is a fantastic tool for creating a buzz around your event. Utilize high-quality images and videos to capture the essence of your event and showcase its unique features. Use event-related hashtags, such as the event name or theme, to increase discoverability and reach a broader audience. Encourage attendees to share their own photos and experiences using a branded event hashtag, allowing their content to become a part of the event's narrative. Engage with users by liking and commenting on their posts and consider partnering with relevant influencers who can promote your event to their dedicated followers.

2. Email marketing campaigns

When it comes to event promotion, email marketing campaigns can be highly effective in reaching a wide audience. By building a subscriber list, you can have a direct line of communication with potential attendees. Building a subscriber list involves creating engaging opt-in forms on your website, offering incentives for sign-ups, and promoting your email list on social media platforms. Crafting compelling email content is essential to capture the attention of your subscribers. Write personalized and engaging emails, showcasing the unique aspects of your event, including key details, highlights, and exclusive offers. Furthermore, optimizing email delivery ensures that your emails reach the intended recipients' inboxes. Avoid spam filters by using reputable email marketing platforms, optimizing the layout of your emails, and regularly reviewing your email performance metrics.

2.1. Building a subscriber list

Building a subscriber list is a crucial step in conducting successful email marketing campaigns for event promotion. Start by creating eye-catching opt-in forms on your website that encourage visitors to subscribe to your email updates. Offering incentives such as exclusive discounts or timely access to event details can entice people to join your list. Additionally, leverage your social media following by promoting your email list through posts and ads. Encourage your existing subscribers to share your emails with their friends and colleagues who might be interested in attending your event. Consistently growing your subscriber list will ensure a wider outreach for your email campaigns.

2.2. Crafting compelling email content

When crafting email content for your event marketing campaigns, aim to create engaging and personalized messages that resonate with your subscribers. Start with a catchy subject line that grabs attention and entices recipients to open the email. Use captivating visuals, such as high-quality event photos or videos, to make your emails visually appealing. Personalize the content by addressing recipients by name and tailoring the message to their interests and preferences. Highlight the unique aspects of your event, such as featured speakers, exclusive experiences, or special promotions. Do not forget to include clear and enticing calls to action, directing recipients to register or learn more about the event.

2.3. Optimizing email delivery

To ensure your carefully crafted emails reach your subscribers' inboxes, optimizing email delivery is essential. Begin by using a reputable email marketing platform that has strong deliverability rates and built-in anti-spam measures. Pay attention to email formatting and design, ensuring that your emails are visually appealing, mobile-friendly, and free from broken links. Regularly monitor your email performance metrics, including open rates, click-through rates, and bounce rates, to identify any potential issues. Segment your email list based on recipients' preferences or demographics to target specific groups effectively. By continuously refining your email delivery strategy, your event promotions will have a higher chance of successfully reaching the intended audience.

3. Collaborating with influencers

Collaborating with influencers can boost the visibility and attendance of your event. By leveraging the influence of individuals who have a large following and are relevant to your target audience, you can tap into their network and broaden the reach of your event promotion efforts. Influencers can include popular bloggers, social media personalities, industry experts, or celebrities. By partnering with influencers, you can benefit from their credibility and trust, and increase the chances of attracting more attendees to your event.

3.1. Identifying relevant influencers

Identifying relevant influencers is a crucial step in collaborating effectively. Start by researching individuals or accounts that have a significant following within your target audience. Look for influencers who have a strong online presence, engage with their followers, and create content related to your event's industry or theme. Consider factors like their reach, engagement rate, and the alignment of their content with your event's objectives. Tools like social media analytics platforms can help you analyze the impact and relevance of potential influencers, ensuring a targeted and effective partnership.

3.2. Establishing partnerships

Once you have identified relevant influencers, it is time to establish partnerships. Reach out to them through direct messages or email, introducing your event and expressing your interest in collaborating. Clearly communicate the benefits for both parties, such as exposure to a new audience or exclusive content opportunities. Personalize your approach to demonstrate that you have done your research and genuinely value their influence. Building relationships with influencers is essential, so consider offering them incentives like VIP access or exclusive rewards to further motivate their involvement.

3.3. Leveraging influencer reach

When collaborating with influencers, it is important to leverage their reach to maximize the impact of your event promotion. Provide influencers with engaging and shareable content, such as sneak peeks, behind-the-scenes footage, or exclusive announcements. Encourage them to actively participate by posting about your event on their social media channels, sharing personalized discount codes, or hosting giveaways for their followers. This not only increases visibility but also creates buzz and excitement around your event, attracting more potential attendees who trust and follow the influencer's recommendations.

3.4. Measuring influencer impact

Measuring the impact of your collaboration with influencers is crucial for evaluating its success and making informed decisions for future events. Track key metrics such as website traffic, social media engagement, ticket sales, or event registrations during and after the influencer partnership. Use unique tracking URLs, promo codes, or dedicated landing pages to monitor conversions and attribution to influencer-driven efforts. Analyze the data to identify which influencers generated the highest engagement, conversions, or overall ROI. This evaluation will help you refine your influencer selection and optimize your strategies for future event promotional campaigns.

4. Utilizing event listing platforms

One effective strategy to promote your event is by utilizing event listing platforms. These platforms provide a centralized location for people to discover and learn about upcoming events in their area. By listing your event on these platforms, you can reach a wider audience and increase the chances of attracting attendees. Additionally, event listing platforms often offer features such as event recommendations and personalized notifications, allowing you to target your ideal audience effectively.

4.1. Researching popular event listing websites

When utilizing event listing platforms, it is essential to research and identify popular event listing websites. Popular event listing websites have a large user base and attract a considerable number of eventgoers. By listing your event on these websites, you can increase visibility and reach a broader audience. Some popular event listing websites include Eventbrite, Meetup, and Eventful. However, it is important to choose websites that are relevant to your event's niche to ensure that you are targeting the right audience.

4.2. Optimizing event listings

To maximize the impact of your event listings on event listing platforms, it is crucial to optimize them. Start by creating attention-grabbing titles and compelling descriptions that clearly communicate the unique aspects and benefits of attending your event. Use keywords related to your event's theme or topic to increase search visibility. Additionally, include relevant information such as date, time, location, and ticket prices. Use high-quality images or videos to capture potential attendees' attention and make your event stand out from the crowd.

4.3. Encouraging attendee reviews

Encouraging attendee reviews is an effective way to promote your event and build credibility. Positive reviews can attract more attendees and generate excitement for future events. After your event, encourage attendees to leave reviews on event listing platforms. Prompt them to share their experiences, highlight the highlights of the event, and provide feedback. Respond to reviews, both positive and negative, to show that you value attendee opinions and are committed to improving future events. Additionally, you can offer incentives such as discounts or exclusive access to encourage attendees to submit reviews.

Chapter 41

How to Market an Event

Events are a wonderful way to engage your customers — except when no one shows up. To make sure you do not end up with an empty room full of balloons, follow some of these best practices:

Capitalize on holidays and special occasions.

Things like New Year's, Small Business Saturday, the finale of a popular TV show, or anything that is collectively on people's minds, can help you land on a theme for your event and create excitement. Try to get creative, too. For example, if you host a Mad Men finale party, put midcentury furniture on sale as a fun twist. (Note: no Mad Men event is complete without some cocktails.)

Old-school signage

Yes, it is the digital age (more on that below), but physical signs are also an effective way to market your event — especially if a lot of foot traffic passes by your store window. Another thing to consider is flyers. For this strategy, think about where your customers are likely to be receptive to your event. An esthetician offering a class on the best foods for healthy skin, for example, might ask a neighborhood yoga studio if it would be willing to put up some flyers.

Tap your neighborhood.

It is always a clever idea to extend invitations to fellow neighborhood businesses. For one, it brings the neighborhood together, fostering a sense of community. And, if they know about your event, they may be more likely to tell their customers about it, too.

Email marketing.

Sending your customers an email about your event is a lever you will always want to pull. Luckily, Customer Engagement [1] has a ready-to-go template that's specifically tailored for marketing events. What is great about Customer Engagement is that it automatically segments your customers into three groups — loyal, casual, and lapsed. So, you could invite just your most loyal customers to an event you want to keep intimate, for example.

Social media

If you have a robust social media presence, market your event there. And if your event is around a holiday, be sure to include relevant hashtags (#FathersDay, for example). That will get you in the stream of conversation. You can also

---

1.   https://squareup.com/customer-engagement

directly @ mention some of your most engaged followers on Twitter. Things like "hope to see you there!" go a long way in making them feel special. Another social media best practice is to post pictures of the event after it is over, tagging the customers who were there (if you have their social info). This wraps things up nicely and has the added benefit of letting the social sphere know that your store is a fun place to be.

Think about timing.

People are busy, so it is good to let them know about things earlier rather than later. If you are sending them an email invitation using Square's email templates, try to do it a few weeks before the big day. Then a few days before, send a reminder.

Send follow-up notes.

After the event is over, do not go radio silent. You might want to send them a discount as a token of appreciation for making your event so special. Customer Engagement has another template specifically tailored for discounts, so you can easily put that to use.

Capture people's contact information.

Aside from being a fun way to bring your customers together, events are also a great opportunity to capture more people's contact information. Ask new folks for their contact info so you can build your Customer Directory. Then you can easily send them updates about your business, or even invite them to your next event.

Chapter42

How to Promote a Festival

1. Online Promotion

Festivals are a wonderful way to bring money into a community and get locals excited about an upcoming event. To effectively promote a festival online, there are several strategies that can be employed. Creating a festival website is essential as it serves as a central hub of information for attendees. The website should include details about the festival, such as the lineup, schedule, ticketing information, and any additional attractions. Social media platforms should also be utilized to reach a wider audience. By creating engaging posts, sharing updates, and encouraging followers to share content, festivals can attract more participants. Collaborating with influencers and bloggers in the festival's niche can also help increase exposure and generate buzz. Their endorsements and reviews can reach a larger audience and generate interest in attending the festival.

1.1. Create a festival website.

Creating a festival website is an essential part of promoting a festival online. The website serves as the central hub of information for festivalgoers, providing details about the event, such as the lineup, schedule, ticketing information, and any additional attractions. It should have a visually appealing design that reflects the festival's theme and brand. Valuable information should be easily accessible, and the website should be mobile-friendly to cater to a larger audience. To further engage attendees, interactive features like online ticket purchasing, forums, and photo galleries can be included. Additionally, integrating social media links on the website allows visitors to share festival details with their network, spreading the word further.

1.2. Utilize social media platforms.

Social media platforms provide a powerful tool for promoting festivals and reaching a wider audience. Creating official festival pages on platforms like Facebook, Instagram, and Twitter allows organizers to share updates, engage with followers, and build excitement. Festivals should consistently post engaging content, such as artist announcements, behind-the-scenes glimpses, and interactive polls or contests, to keep followers entertained and informed. Utilizing event hashtags and encouraging attendees to share their festival experiences on social media can also help generate buzz. It is important to monitor and respond to comments, messages, and mentions on social media to ensure a positive online presence and address any inquiries or concerns.

1.3. Collaborate with influencers and bloggers.

Collaborating with influencers and bloggers in the festival's niche is an effective way to promote the event and increase its visibility. These individuals have established audiences who trust their recommendations and opinions. By partnering with relevant influencers and bloggers, festivals can leverage their reach and tap into their follower base to generate interest and ticket sales. Organizers can invite influencers to attend the festival as special guests or brand ambassadors, offering them VIP or backstage access in exchange for social media coverage and promotional content. Bloggers can also be approached to write sponsored posts or reviews about the festival, highlighting its unique aspects and attractions. Such collaborations can significantly amplify the festival's online presence and attract a larger audience.

2. Offline Promotion

Festivals are not only promoted online, but offline promotions are equally important to reach a wider audience. Offline promotion strategies can help create awareness among locals and generate excitement about the upcoming event. Some effective offline promotion methods include distributing flyers and posters throughout the community, partnering with local businesses for cross-promotion, advertising in local newspapers and radio stations to reach a broader demographic, and hosting pre-festival events to generate buzz and build anticipation. By utilizing these offline promotion tactics, festival organizers can ensure maximum visibility and engagement from the local community.

2.1. Distribute flyers and posters.

Distributing flyers and posters is a traditional yet effective way to promote a festival. Design eye-catching flyers and posters that showcase the festival's key highlights and dates. Distribute them at popular gathering spots in the community, such as coffee shops, libraries, and community centers. Additionally, collaborate with local businesses to display flyers and posters in their establishments. This way, the festival information will reach a larger audience, increasing the chances of attracting more attendees and creating a buzz around the event.

2.2. Partner with local businesses

Partnering with local businesses is a win-win strategy for promoting a festival and supporting the community. Identify businesses in the area that align with the festival's theme or target audience and establish partnerships. The festival can offer promotional opportunities to local businesses such as featuring their logos on the festival website, providing booth spaces for them to showcase their products or services, or offering exclusive discounts or packages to their customers. In return, the festival gains the support and promotion from these local businesses, widening its reach and attracting more attendees.

2.3. Advertise in local newspapers and radio stations.

Advertising in local newspapers and radio stations significantly helps in reaching a broader local audience. Contact the editorial or advertising departments of local newspapers to inquire about advertising options for the festival. Place ads in both print and online editions to maximize exposure. Similarly, collaborate with local radio stations to have festival announcements, interviews, or promotions aired regularly. Radio ads and mentions can attract the attention of potential attendees who may not be active online, ensuring that the festival's message reaches a diverse range of people within the community.

2.4. Host pre-festival events.

To build excitement and generate anticipation, hosting pre-festival events is a fantastic way to engage the community and create a buzz around the upcoming festival. Organize smaller-scale events leading up to the main festival, such as pre-festival concerts, art exhibitions, or workshops related to the festival's theme. These events can act as teasers for the main festival while allowing attendees to experience a taste of what's to come. Additionally, use these pre-festival events as platforms to announce and promote the main festival, encouraging attendees to spread the word and invite others to join the festivities.

3. Engaging the Community

Engaging in the community is key to promoting a festival successfully. By involving the local community, you can generate excitement and encourage participation. One effective way to engage the community is to organize contests and giveaways. This could include social media contests where participants have the chance to win festival tickets or merchandise. Contests not only generate buzz, but also create a sense of anticipation among locals who are eager to participate and potentially win exciting prizes.

3.1. Organize contests and giveaways.

Organizing contests and giveaways is a fantastic way to engage the community and promote your festival. Offering exciting prizes such as VIP passes, merchandise, or even exclusive meet-and-greet opportunities can create a buzz and generate interest. Social media platforms are an ideal way to host these contests and

giveaways, allowing participants to easily enter and share with their friends. By utilizing hashtags and encouraging user-generated content, you can expand the reach of the contests and increase visibility for your festival.

3.2. Encourage local participation.

Encouraging local participation is vital to the success of a festival and strengthens the sense of community. One way to achieve this is by involving local artists, performers, and businesses in the event. Providing opportunities for local talent to showcase their skills, whether through performances or art installations, not only adds value to the festival but also creates a sense of pride among the community. Collaborating with local businesses to sponsor or host festival-related events can also foster a stronger bond between the festival and the community, leading to increased support and attendance.

3.3. Offer exclusive discounts and promotions.

Offering exclusive discounts and promotions is a wonderful way to incentivize the local community to attend the festival. Creating exclusive discounts for residents or businesses can help generate excitement and encourage ticket sales. Early bird discounts, group discounts, or limited-time promotions can entice potential attendees to secure their spots early. Additionally, partnering with local businesses to provide festival-related discounts or promotions, such as discounts at nearby restaurants or shops, can further encourage engagement and increase attendance, benefiting both the festival and the local economy.

4. Building Excitement

Building excitement is crucial to ensure a successful festival. One effective strategy is to tease festival highlights on social media. Utilize platforms like Facebook, Instagram, and Twitter to share enticing snippets, such as sneak peeks of headlining performers, unique attractions, or special activities. Create captivating posts, videos, and images that give a taste of what attendees can expect. This creates anticipation and generates a buzz among potential festivalgoers, encouraging them to mark their calendars and spread the word about the event.

4.1. Tease festival highlights on social media.

Social media is a powerful tool for promoting festivals. A great tactic to build excitement is to tease festival highlights on these platforms. Share intriguing details about the festival lineup, special performances, or unique experiences attendees can look forward to. Post engaging content like short interviews with artists, behind-

the-scenes glimpses, or teasers of festival preparations. Encourage followers to like, comment, and share to expand the reach. By creating a sense of anticipation and

exclusivity, you can pique the interest of potential attendees and enhance their excitement for the upcoming festival.

4.2. Create a countdown campaign.

Adding a countdown campaign can significantly amplify anticipation for your festival. Start the countdown on social media, your festival website, and through email newsletters. Highlight the number of days left until the event and unveil exciting surprises, announcements, or contests periodically as the countdown progresses. Encourage followers to tag their friends, share the countdown, and engage in discussions about what they are most excited. This creates a sense of urgency, builds momentum, and keeps the festival at the forefront of people's minds as the date approaches, generating buzz and excitement among potential attendees.

4.3. Showcase past festival memories.

One powerful way to build excitement for a festival is to showcase memorable moments from past editions. Share captivating photos and videos of highlights such as energetic performances, stunning decorations, and joyful crowds. Highlight the unique experiences and create a sense of nostalgia among your audience. Encourage festivalgoers to share their own favorite memories, creating a sense of community and fostering anticipation for the upcoming event. By reminding people of the incredible experiences they can have at the festival, you reignite their enthusiasm and encourage them to attend again and share the festival with others.

4.4. Collaborate with local artists and performers.

Collaborating with local artists and performers can contribute to building excitement for your festival. Partner with talented individuals from the community who can showcase their skills and entertain the attendees. This could include musicians, dancers, visual artists, or even theatrical performers. Promote these collaborations through social media, interviews, and sneak peeks to generate interest and curiosity among both the artists' fanbase and the general audience. By involving local talents, you not only create a diverse and unique festival experience but also establish a strong connection with the community and increase the festival's appeal, attracting a broader audience.

Chapter 43

Internet Concert

1. Introduction

Internet concerts have revolutionized the way artists connect with their fans. With the advancement of technology, it is now possible to perform live stream performances and engage with audiences worldwide. This has opened new opportunities for musicians, bands, and artists to showcase their talent, expand their fan base, and create unforgettable experiences. Through platforms like Ustream.com, individuals can easily broadcast their concerts online, providing an immersive and interactive experience for fans who can join from the comfort of their own homes.

1.1 What is Ustream.com?

Ustream.com is a live interactive broadcast platform that enables individuals to connect with their fans in real-time. It allows anyone with an internet connection and a camera to start engaging with their audience, regardless of their location. Whether you are a musician, comedian, or public speaker, Ustream.com offers a user-friendly interface that facilitates live streaming of events. By harnessing the power of the internet, Ustream.com breaks down barriers, allowing artists to reach a global audience and create virtual concert experiences.

1.2 Benefits of Ustream.com

Ustream.com brings numerous benefits to artists and performers looking to host internet concerts. Firstly, it provides a platform that is easily accessible to both performers and fans, allowing for seamless communication and engagement. Additionally, Ustream.com offers a scalable streaming solution, ensuring that no matter the size of the audience, the quality of the live stream will remain high. The platform also enables artists to monetize their concerts through ticket sales or sponsored content. With Ustream.com, artists can expand their reach and connect with fans on a global scale, all while maintaining full control over their performance and creative vision.

2. Planning an Internet Concert

Planning an Internet concert requires careful consideration and organization to ensure a successful event. From choosing the right venue to promoting the event, each step plays a crucial role in creating an engaging experience for fans. It is important to plan and have an unobstructed vision of the concert's objectives, target audience, and desired outcome. By following a structured plan, artists can effectively leverage the power of Ustream.com to connect with their fans and deliver an entertaining performance.

2.1 Choosing the Right Venue

Choosing the right venue for an Internet concert is essential to create the desired atmosphere and enhance the overall experience for the audience. Factors such as acoustics, lighting, and seating capacity should be considered. Additionally, considering the technical requirements for streaming the concert live on Ustream.com is crucial. Finding a venue that can provide reliable internet connectivity and suitable audiovisual equipment is paramount to ensure smooth broadcasting. By selecting a venue that aligns with the artist's style and requirements, the Internet concert can leave an impression on the virtual audience.

2.2 Setting Up the Equipment

Setting up the equipment for an Internet concert involves preparing the necessary audio, video, and streaming devices. This includes ensuring the cameras are positioned at optimal angles, the microphones capture high-quality sound, and the streaming software is properly configured. Testing the equipment beforehand is vital to identify any technical issues and make any necessary adjustments. It is important to have backup equipment available in case of unforeseen failures. By carefully setting up the equipment, artists can deliver a seamless and professional performance to their online audience.

2.3 Promoting the Event

Promoting the Internet concert is crucial to attract a wider audience and increase engagement. Utilizing various promotional channels such as social media, email newsletters, and artist websites can help spread the word about the upcoming event. Creating visually appealing graphics, teaser videos, and event announcements can generate excitement and anticipation among fans. Collaborating with influencers or utilizing online advertising can also amplify the reach of the promotion. By implementing effective promotional strategies, artists can ensure that their Internet concert garners the attention it deserves and maximizes fan participation.

3. Engaging with Fans during an Internet Concert

An internet concert provides a unique opportunity for artists to directly engage with their fans in real-time. By taking advantage of live chat features, artists can interact with their audience, creating a more intimate and personal experience. Through live chat, fans can share their excitement, ask questions, and even share their favorite songs or moments from the concert. This direct interaction allows artists to connect with their fans on a deeper level and build a keen sense of community.

3.1 Interacting through Live Chat

Live chat is an essential tool for artists to engage with their fans during an internet concert. It enables real-time communication, allowing fans to express their thoughts, emotions, and enthusiasm during the concert. Artists can use the live chat to address the audience, acknowledge their comments, and respond to their questions. It adds an interactive element to the concert experience, making fans feel like they are part of something special and creating a more personal connection between the artist and their audience.

3.2 Taking Audience Requests

Taking audience requests is a fantastic way to involve fans in an internet concert. Artists can encourage their audience to suggest songs they want to hear, creating a sense of anticipation and excitement. By incorporating these requests into the concert's setlist, artists can show their appreciation for their fans and make the experience more personalized. It also allows fans to feel like they have a direct impact on the concert, making it a unique and memorable event for everyone involved.

3.3 Encouraging Fan Participation

Fan participation is a key aspect of an internet concert. Artists can encourage fans to actively participate by organizing contests or interactive elements during the event. This can include trivia questions, polls, or even inviting fans to join the stage for a song or performance. By providing opportunities for fans to actively engage, artists can create a sense of excitement and make the concert feel like a collaborative experience between the artist and their fans. It fosters a keen sense of loyalty and connection, leaving fans eager to attend future internet concerts.

3.4 Handling Technical Difficulties

While technical difficulties are always a possibility during an internet concert, artists can be prepared to handle them effectively. It is crucial to have a backup plan in case of any technical issues, such as having alternative streaming platforms ready or a dedicated technical support team. Artists should communicate transparently with their fans if any difficulties arise, providing updates and troubleshooting advice to minimize disruptions. By being proactive and responsive, artists can ensure the best possible concert experience for their fans, even when unexpected technical challenges occur.

4. Post-Concert Activities

After the internet concert is over, there are several important post-concert activities to consider. These activities help to extend the reach and impact of the concert beyond the live event. They include sharing the concert recording, collecting feedback from fans, and planning future internet concerts. By engaging in these activities, artists can continue to connect with their fans and build a loyal fan base.

4.1 Sharing the Concert Recording

Sharing the concert recording is a wonderful way to give fans who missed the live event an opportunity to experience the concert. By uploading the recording to platforms like Ustream.com, fans can relive the excitement and energy of the concert at their convenience. Artists can also share the recording on social media platforms and their website to reach a wider audience. Additionally, offering the concert recording for sale or as a free download can generate additional revenue and help promote future internet concerts.

4.2 Collecting Feedback from Fans

Collecting feedback from fans is crucial for artists to understand their audience's experience and make improvements for future internet concerts. Artists can use various methods to collect feedback, such as surveys, social media polls, or encouraging fans to leave comments or reviews. This feedback can provide valuable insights into what aspects of the concert worked well and what can be improved. It also allows artists to address any concerns or issues raised by fans, showing that their opinions are valued.

4.3 Planning Future Internet Concerts

Planning future internet concerts is an essential part of building a successful online presence as an artist. By analyzing the feedback received from fans, artists can identify areas of improvement and incorporate them into the planning process. They can explore different themes, setlists, or even collaborate with other artists for future concerts to keep the audience engaged and excited. Planning future internet concerts also involves promoting the events in advance to build anticipation and ensure a larger turnout. By continuously planning and delivering high-quality internet concerts, artists can strengthen their fan base and reach new audiences.

Chapter 44

Event Checklist: At Least One Week Before

Put up posters around town. Do not rely completely on social media and the Internet to promote your band. An eye-catching flyer or poster is another wonderful way to grab attention and bring people out to your show.

- **Step up promotion on social media.** Share and re-share your Facebook event and a digital image of your flyer or poster, and make sure you have invited all your local friends and followers.

- **Contact local bloggers, radio personalities, and alt-weekly writers.** If you can get a little media coverage for your gig, you will be able to reach new fans. Plus, you can share the coverage you get on social media to keep your current fans engaged and excited. Look for people who specialize in covering local music or music in your genre to help you out.

- **Send an email to your local fans.** You have noticed that it is hard to reach all your fans on Facebook. For that reason, it's a great idea to have an email list[1], as well. When you have a big show coming up, you can be sure your fans will get your email. The same cannot be said for your Facebook posts.

---

1. http://diymusician.cdbaby.com/musician-tips/12-ways-build-email-list/

- **Confirm advance information with the venue.** Make sure you know what time you need to set up, how long your set is, and the terms for payment have been agreed upon.

The Day Before

- **Double-check your gear.** Do all your cables work? Do you need new strings? Better to take care of those things now than have an equipment issue on stage.

- **Pack your gig bag[2].** I like to bring a bottle of water, a couple of protein bars, a roll of duct tape, extra ear plugs, sharpies, spare guitar strings, a handful of guitar picks, a bottle of hand sanitizer, and a small notebook with me to each show. Pack your bag the day before to get it out of the way and reduce stress the day of the show.

- **Print or write copies of your setlist.** Do not wing it on stage. Make sure you have planned your set and practiced it before your show.

- **Plan your outfit.** Figure out what you want to wear and lay it out somewhere. Do not add stress by scrambling to find the right stage, look at the very last minute. If you are in a band or ensemble, talk about what you are going to wear with the group so you can present a cohesive image.

---

2.   http://takelessons.com/blog/electric-guitar-accessories-gig

- **Get a good night's sleep.** You will perform better when you are rested, and you will have more fun.

The Day Of

- **Banish your stage fright** [3] **with a calming activity.** Get into a good mindset by reading a book, meditating, exercising, or watching your favorite show. Figure out what calms you and helps you prepare to play like the rockstar you are.

- **Eat a light meal two to three hours before you perform.** When you are on stage, you do not want to feel heavy and sleepy like you have just eaten five Thanksgiving dinners, but you also do not want to get hungry and lightheaded. Have a healthy meal so you will be on top of your game.

At the Gig

- **Be there on time.** Being punctual shows the venue that you respect their time, appreciate the opportunity you have been given to perform, and that you are professional. Seriously, if you do not follow any of these other tips, you must at least show up on time.

- **Always be polite and professional.** Save your complaints about the crowd, venue, or other

---

3.   http://takelessons.com/blog/open-mic-how-to-overcome-stage-fright

bands for the privacy of your rehearsal space. When you are at the gig, be positive and kind. You never know who is watching, and you want to make a great impression.

- **Say 'hi' to the sound person** and remember their name. The sound guy or gal is the person who has the biggest impact on how you will sound in the audience. Be nice to them, and always remember to thank them for their help.

- **Make friends with the other bands.** Hang out and watch their seats, and they will want to stay for yours, too. If you are lucky, the other bands will like you and offer you another great gig.

- **Do not forget to bring merch.** One of the best ways to make money at a gig is to have something for sale. Additionally, people will remember you better if they have something to take with them. Whether you have stickers and CDs or vinyl records and T-shirts, do not play a show without putting something on the merch table.

- **Always thank the venue, the fans, and the other bands during your set.** Be gracious and spread the love. Being likable will help you get further in your local music scene than just talent alone.

- **Have fun on stage!!!** Enjoy your time in the spotlight. Your audience will feel the vibes and have a wonderful time, too.

The Next Day

- **Post thank you on social media to your fans, the other bands, and the venue.** Keep the good times rolling by thanking everyone again. They will notice and appreciate it.

- **Re-post the photos that your fans shared at the gig.** If someone captured a great live shot of you, show other people what they missed by sharing it. You can generate buzz for your next show by sharing how much fun your show was last night.

- **Update the upcoming gigs list on your website.** Make sure your concert listings stay current by updating your site the next day.

Once the gig has come and gone, remember that the most important thing is the music. Keep practicing and working on your craft, whether you have a show coming up or not. You can always improve musically[4], and you'll likely find you get better with every gig you play.

---

4.   https://takelessons.com/

music-lessons?utm_source=blog-student&utm_medium=content&utm_campaign=tl-blog

Chapter 45

Event Marketing Plan

1. Importance of Event Marketing

Event marketing plays a crucial role in the success of any event. It is the key to spreading awareness about the event and generating excitement among the target audience. Without effective marketing, the event may go unnoticed and fail to attract attendees. By creating a marketing plan, organizers can strategically promote the event, engage potential attendees, and ensure its success. Marketing is essential for building brand recognition, generating interest, and driving ticket sales and increasing attendance.

1.1. Spreading the Word

Spreading the word about an event is vital to its success. It involves using various channels and mediums to reach as many people as possible. Social media platforms, online communities, and word-of-mouth are great ways to create buzz and generate interest. By leveraging these channels, organizers can share event details, build anticipation, and encourage potential attendees to spread the word further. Effective event marketing requires compelling messaging, visually appealing content, and consistent communication to capture the attention of the target audience.

1.2. Selling Tickets

Selling tickets is a primary goal of event marketing. The marketing plan should include strategies to entice potential attendees to purchase tickets. This can be achieved through effective pricing strategies, early bird discounts, limited time offers, or exclusive rewards for early registrants. By highlighting the value and unique experiences that the event offers, organizers can create a sense of urgency and drive ticket sales. Implementing clear and user-friendly ticket purchasing processes, along with seamless payment options, can also contribute to maximizing ticket sales.

1.3. Increasing Attendance

Increasing attendance is a crucial aspect of event marketing. While selling tickets is important, it is equally essential to attract more attendees to make the event successful and memorable. Organizers can leverage various marketing strategies to boost attendance, such as targeted promotions to specific demographics, collaborations with influencers or local businesses, and utilizing online event directories to reach a wider audience. By creating engaging content, fostering a sense of community, and showcasing the unique offerings of the event, organizers can encourage more people to attend and make the event a resounding success.

2. Key Elements of an Event Marketing Plan

When creating an event marketing plan, there are several key elements to consider. These include identifying your target audience, setting marketing goals, choosing marketing channels, and creating compelling content. By focusing on these elements, you can ensure that your event reaches the right people, meets its objectives, effectively utilizes various marketing channels, and engages attendees with captivating content.

2.1. Target Audience Identification

Identifying your target audience is vital in event marketing. It involves understanding the demographics, psychographics, and preferences of the audience you want to attract. By conducting market research, analyzing data, and using audience segmentation techniques, you can pinpoint the specific individuals or groups that are most likely to be interested in attending your event. This allows you to tailor your marketing efforts to resonate with their needs, interests, and motivations, maximizing the chances of attracting and engaging your desired audience.

2.2. Setting Marketing Goals

Setting marketing goals is crucial for the success of your event marketing plan. These goals should be specific, measurable, achievable, relevant, and time-bound (SMART). Whether it is increasing ticket sales, raising brand awareness, expanding your audience reach, or generating leads, having clear and well-defined goals helps guide your marketing strategies and tactics. By setting benchmarks, tracking progress, and regularly evaluating your performance, you can adjust your efforts as needed and measure the success of your event marketing initiatives.

2.3. Choosing Marketing Channels

Choosing the right marketing channels is essential for effectively promoting your event. Consider the preferences and habits of your target audience, as well as the channels that align with your marketing goals. These channels can vary from social media platforms, email marketing, influencer partnerships, collaborations with local businesses, to online event directories. By selecting the most suitable channels, you can optimize your reach, engagement, and conversions, ensuring that your event message reaches the right audience through the most impactful channels.

2.4. Creating Compelling Content

Creating compelling content is a key aspect of event marketing. Your content should be engaging, informative, and persuasive to capture the attention and interest of your target audience. This can include well-crafted event descriptions, enticing visuals, impactful videos, testimonials from previous attendees, and interactive elements. By providing valuable and unique content, you can create a sense of anticipation and excitement around your event, convincing potential attendees that it is an experience they do not want to miss.

3. Strategies for Effective Event Marketing

When it comes to effective event marketing, there are several strategies you can employ to ensure your event gets the attention it deserves. Social media promotion is a vital tool in reaching a wide audience. By leveraging platforms like Facebook, Twitter, and Instagram, you can create compelling posts, share event details, and connect with potential attendees. Influencer partnerships are another powerful strategy. Collaborating with popular influencers in your industry can help you increase your event's visibility and credibility. Email marketing campaigns are also effective in reaching your target audience. By crafting personalized and engaging emails, you can keep potential attendees informed and excited about your event. In addition, collaborating with local businesses can provide mutually beneficial opportunities for cross-promotion. Lastly, utilizing online event directories, such as Eventbrite or Meetup, can help you reach a larger audience and attract attendees who are specifically interested in events like yours.

3.1. Social Media Promotion

Social media promotion is a crucial component of any event marketing plan. With numerous platforms at your disposal, you can leverage their wide reach and engage your target audience effectively. Creating engaging and shareable content is essential for success. Make sure to post visually appealing graphics, videos, and event updates. Utilize relevant hashtags to increase discoverability and encourage attendees to share their content with their followers. Engage with your audience by responding to comments and direct messages promptly. Additionally, consider running paid advertising campaigns on platforms like Facebook and Instagram to extend your reach and target specific audiences. Remember to monitor your analytics and adjust your strategy accordingly to optimize your social media promotion efforts.

3.2. Influencer Partnerships

Influencer partnerships can significantly amplify your event's reach and impact. Identify influential individuals within your industry or niche who have a strong following and align with your event's target audience. Reach out to them with a personalized pitch, highlighting the value they can bring to their audience by promoting your event. In exchange, offer them complimentary tickets or other exclusive rewards. Collaborate with influencers on social media takeovers, sponsored posts, or even speaking engagements at your event. Their endorsement and reach can generate buzz, increase ticket sales, and enhance your event's credibility. Keep track of the results and consider building long-term relationships with influencers to leverage their influence for future events.

3.3. Email Marketing Campaigns

Email marketing campaigns remain a powerful tool for event promotion. Build a targeted email list by capturing leads through your website, social media, or partnerships. Craft compelling and personalized email content that highlights the unique benefits and features of your event. Use eye-catching subject lines to grab attention and consider segmenting your email list to send tailored messages to diverse groups of recipients. Include clear calls-to-action, such as registration links or discounted ticket offers, to encourage click-throughs and conversions. Do not forget to track your email campaign metrics, such as open rates and click-through rates, to gauge the effectiveness of your messaging and make necessary adjustments to optimize your campaign's success.

3.4. Collaborating with Local Businesses

Collaborating with local businesses can be a win-win strategy for event marketing. Seek out partnerships with businesses or organizations that share a similar target audience or have complementary offerings. By cross promoting each other's events or products, you can reach a wider customer base and increase brand awareness. Consider hosting joint promotions, sharing each other's social media posts, or even co-hosting events. Tap into their existing customer base and leverage their relationships within the community. This collaborative approach strengthens community connections and adds credibility to your event. Establishing local business partnerships can also provide opportunities to access resources, venues, or special promotions that can enhance your event's overall experience.

3.5. Utilizing Online Event Directories

Online event directories offer a valuable platform for promoting your event to a targeted audience actively seeking relevant experiences. Listing your event on popular directories like Eventbrite, Meetup, or local event listing websites can significantly increase your event's exposure. Ensure your event listing includes compelling descriptions, eye-catching visuals, and relevant keywords to attract potential attendees. Take advantage of the promotional tools provided by these directories, such as featured listings or sponsored placements, to increase visibility. Encourage attendees to leave reviews or ratings on the directories after the event to further promote your event's success and attract future attendees. Regularly update your event page with added information, engaging content, and any changes to keep your listing fresh and enticing.

4. Measuring and Analyzing Event Marketing Success

Measuring and analyzing the success of your event marketing efforts is crucial to understand what worked and what did not. By tracking different metrics, you can gain valuable insights into the effectiveness of your strategies and make data-driven decisions for future events. This process involves assessing ticket sales, social media engagement, email campaign metrics, and gathering attendee feedback. By closely examining these key indicators, you can evaluate the overall impact of your marketing efforts and identify areas for improvement. Effective analysis allows you to refine your event marketing plan and achieve better results with each event you organize.

4.1. Tracking Ticket Sales

Tracking ticket sales is an essential part of measuring the success of your event marketing plan. By monitoring the number of tickets sold, you can evaluate the effectiveness of your promotional strategies and pricing tactics. This data helps you understand the demand for your event and identify any patterns or trends in ticket purchases. Additionally, tracking sales allows you to estimate attendance and make necessary adjustments to optimize the event experience. Whether it is monitoring online ticket platforms or analyzing sales reports, keeping a close eye on ticket sales provides valuable information for assessing the effectiveness of your event marketing efforts.

4.2. Monitoring Social Media Engagement

In today's digital age, social media plays a pivotal role in event marketing success. Monitoring social media engagement allows you to assess the impact of your promotional activities across different platforms. By tracking metrics such as likes, shares, comments, and post reach, you can measure the effectiveness of your social media campaigns and identify which content resonates best with your target audience. Analyzing social media engagement also provides insights into the demographic profile and interests of your followers, enabling you to tailor future marketing efforts for better results. Regularly monitoring social media metrics helps you stay connected with your audience and adapt your strategies to maximize engagement and reach.

4.3. Analyzing Email Campaign Metrics

Email marketing campaigns are a powerful tool for event promotion, and analyzing their metrics is key to measuring their success. By examining open rates, click-through rates, and conversions, you can evaluate the effectiveness of your email campaigns in driving ticket sales and generating attendee interest. Understanding which subject lines, content, and visual elements resonate with your audience allows you to refine your email marketing strategy for future events. Additionally, analyzing email campaign metrics provides insights into the engagement levels and preferences of your subscribers, enabling you to create more personalized and targeted communications. This data-driven approach ensures that your event marketing efforts via email are impactful and yield positive results.

4.4. Gathering Attendee Feedback

Gathering feedback from event attendees is a valuable practice to assess the overall success of your event marketing strategy. By implementing surveys, questionnaires, or feedback forms, you can capture valuable insights from attendees regarding their experience, satisfaction, and suggestions for improvement. This feedback enables you to understand attendee preferences, identify strengths and weaknesses of your event, and make informed decisions for future iterations. By actively seeking attendee feedback, you demonstrate that their opinions are valued, creating a stronger connection with your audience, and fostering loyalty. Incorporating attendee feedback into your event marketing plan allows you to continually enhance the event experience and ensure its continued success.

www.ingramcontent.com/pod-product-compliance
Lightning Source LLC
Chambersburg PA
CBHW051216130726
47988CB00001B/111